Tyler G. Hicks

How to
Borrow Your Way
to a Great Fortune

Parker Publishing Company, Inc.   West Nyack, N Y

How to Build Great Wealth Using the Magic of OPM—Other People's Money

You can build great riches quickly, starting with no money of your own if you use the magic growth and leverage powers of OPM—other people's money. This book shows you exactly how and where to borrow OPM and put it to use earning *your* fortune.

Anyone can make a million dollars in a short time if he:

(a) Knows who's ready to lend money
(b) Understands borrowing techniques
(c) Borrows for investment purposes
(d) Puts OPM to work earning his fortune

You can work on a job for 50 years and earn just the bare essentials of life. But take the smart-money course to wealth—a business of your own financed with OPM—and you can make a million within just a few years. In this book I show you hundreds of tried and proven ways to borrow OPM quickly and with the least effort on your part.

But I don't leave you at the bank door or the stockbroker's office with a bundle of money in your hand. I take you, by means of numerous interesting and exciting actual stories, through the best procedures for investing OPM for the maximum profit.

As a creative investor, business builder, idea producer, or speculator, you are *entitled* to use OPM because you have the seeds (ideas, plans, techniques, etc.) which grow the money tree. Many people who have money which they inherited are so uncreative they plead for creative help in putting their dollars profitably to work. Even banks, insurance companies, financial organizations, and stockbrokers are avidly seeking creative people like you to put OPM to work to earn big profits.

As someone who wants to use borrowed money to build wealth, you are unique. Most people just want security—a steady job with regular raises in pay. These people are afraid to take business risks—they seldom, or never, think of borrowing money to make money.

So why shouldn't you, as a special type of person, be entitled to more in life? I firmly believe you deserve more of the good things of this life— wealth, luxury, leisure—and I show you how to obtain them using the glorious magic of OPM.

So come with me, fellow wealth builder, and let's move up the gold-studded wealth road. Success can, and will, be yours—if you use my suggestions and apply my techniques. You can't lose because every technique I recommend to you is a mavelous dollar generator that I use in my daily wealth-building activities. Thousands of others have built quick wealth from small beginnings. You, too, can do the same. Let's get started—right now.

TYLER G. HICKS

Contents

8. How State and Local Loans Can Build Your Wealth
    (*Continued*)

*nize the Size of State Aid • How to Get State or
Local Business Aid • Winning Ways Are Easy to
Learn • You Must See the Whole Picture • Aim
Your Loan Applications at Success • State Funds
Build a Fortune • Train Your Workers Using
State Funds • Put the Five M's to Work • Get
Local Funds, Too • Where to Get Your State
Money • Use These Three Magic Wealth Builders
• Leverage Multiplies Your Capital • Be Wary
of Leverage Risks • Synergy Gives You GO
POWER • Synergy Goes to Work for You •
Serendipity Helps You Find Your Fortune*

*Count Your Business Blessings • Know Your Loan
Sources • What Kinds of Loans Can You Obtain
• Learn SBA Loan Amounts and Rates • Why
Does SBA Reject Loans? • Other Sources of
Federal Funds • How to Be Sure Your Loan Is
Approved • Use Your Friends • Reach for the
Big Money • Accentuate Your Skills • Bring
Uncle Sam into Your Business • Great Success
Can Be Yours • Analyze Low-Capital Activities
• You Can Get Good Advice • Stay Out of Busi-
ness Trouble • Have Faith in Uncle Sam •
Don't Be Ashamed to Use Government Money*

*Know the Details of Stock Sales • Advantages
of Going Public • Ten Key Questions on Selling
Stock • How to Sell Your Stock • Be a Big-
Time Winner • Make Yourself a Millionaire •
Make Reg A Work for You • Four Steps to Using*

You Can Borrow Your Way to Great Wealth

Everywhere I go I meet successful, wealthy people. From New York to San Francisco, Los Angeles to Sydney, London to Stockholm, Copenhagen to Rome, San Diego to Tokyo; from east to west and west to east, the story is the same—hundreds and hundreds of happy, successful people.

Were you to travel with me you'd meet these rich people in the best hotels, the finest restaurants, exclusive clubs, and the biggest resorts. What's more, you'd learn a great deal from these outstandingly successful people—I know that I have.

But the *key fact*, the *ultimate secret* that would become yours as the conversation with each person progressed is this:

Nearly every person who built great wealth for himself in recent years did so on borrowed money—that is, he started with little or no money and wound up with a lot of money!

As we traveled from city to city and met person after person you'd soon be convinced that the best way to build a fortune today is by using OPM—other people's money. And your conclusion is correct— OPM is the most powerful key to fast riches known in the world today. Yet few folks know the real ins and outs of using OPM effectively.

Borrowing Is "In"

For years the dream of many folks was to "pay off the mortgage on the house so we'll be free and clear of debt." This was an admirable

17

goal, as was the desire to "save up for a new car and pay cash for it so we can avoid the interest charges of an auto loan."

But times have changed. People are no longer willing to wait long enough to save up for a car, a dishwasher, a color TV. Instead, most people today will borrow the money they need for big-ticket items. They find they can enjoy the car or color TV while they're paying it off. Also, the need to pay off the loan makes them work harder. And almost as important is the fact that the interest cost is easily proven and is tax deductible. So today we find that borrowing is "in"—be the borrower young, middle aged, or older.

Build Wealth by Borrowing

When you buy a car, a washer, a TV, or other personal item using borrowed money you usually just pay out; i.e., the item you buy doesn't return any profit to you other than the pleasure you get from it. In most cases the fun you obtain from your purchase makes the effort to pay for it worthwhile. But you can't use fun to pay grocery bills!

When you borrow money for business purposes, you have a good chance of earning a profit. Unlike the personal car or TV which doesn't pay you anything back, except pleasure, the business investment will often pay you a profit of $50, $100, $200, or more, per week. Now, if you're willing to go into debt to buy something that just costs you *more* money for gas, electricity, etc., and brings you no return but fun, why shouldn't you be willing to borrow money to build wealth?

Check ten people who've hit the big money. Ask them how they got started. In almost every case the answer will be "I borrowed some money from the local bank," or, "My relatives lent me some money— I've paid it all back now."

Learn from Your Best Friend

Count the author of this book as one of your best friends. Why? Because I understand you! No matter how you obtained the copy of the book you're now reading, the fact that you're reading it shows me that you're interested in becoming wealthy. I understand the drive for wealth because I've had it since I was a boy. Since you have a similar wealth drive, I understand you!

Repeat to yourself here and now:

I have a friend who wants me to become wealthy. My friend wants to help me get rich. My friend will help me earn more and I will soon be rich.

Did saying that make you feel more confident? It should, because you have just made a *money friend*. I don't have the time to bowl with you, go on picnics with you, or take vacation trips with you the way your other friends may. But I *do* have the time and desire to take you, step by step, through the world of building wealth using OPM. I want to show you how to get rich starting with *no* capital of your own except some time, energy and the know-how you get from this book.

Why This Book Will Help You

Three of my earlier books dealing with earning money were instant best sellers. Letters and phone calls from readers flooded into my home. The post office stamped thousands of envelopes with the plea *Please Furnish Your Correspondents with Complete Address.* My wife and kids complained about the numerous calls—their friends said our line was *always* busy. The only solution, they said, was an unlisted number.

Of the thousands of calls and letters, fully 90 percent asked one key question—*How, and where, can I borrow the money I need to start, expand, or improve a business?* Note this important fact. These thousands of people had the idea for the business or investment they wanted to go into or make. And, I'm happy to say, most of them had *good, profitable* ideas. They also had plenty of energy, drive, ambition, foresight, and intelligence. The one item they lacked is a five-letter word—MONEY.

Why This Book Was Written

Many of these readers pleaded with me to write a hard-hitting book on how and where they could borrow money for their business. The more I listened and read, the more convinced I became of the great need for such a book. You are now reading that book: a book written to fill *your* needs, a book designed to make you as wealthy as possible, as soon as possible, on borrowed money.

I know you can hit the big money because folks who take time to read books on getting rich usually:

- Have good business ideas
- Are ambitious
- Will take a business risk
- Need OPM to get started

This book *will* help you because it shows you exactly how to borrow the money you need, where to borrow the money, and what to do with the money after you get it.

Now, let's start making you rich using the magic growth power of other people's money. You'll see how you can:

- Borrow money to buy a business
- Watch your business grow
- Take a big salary for yourself
- Pay off your debts
- Own a prosperous business
- Borrow more money to buy bigger businesses
- Build a business empire in just a few years

Use OPM for Other Income

So far we've been talking about using OPM to invest in a business. "But," you say, "I'm not interested in investing in another business. I want to put my money into the stock market or the commodity futures market."

"Fine," I reply. "If you know what you're doing and you have another source of income to pay off any losses you may incur, you can build wealth using borrowed money for stock, bond, commodity, or other purchases. But I want to emphasize as strongly as possible—YOU MUST KNOW WHAT YOU'RE DOING." We'll discuss this aspect in greater detail later in the book.

Why OPM Works Like Magic

Most beginning wealth builders, like you, have super-sensitive financial abilities. Almost every novice fortune seeker I've ever met senses the infinite power of OPM. While some of these wonderful people might have a problem trying to list the magic of OPM, they *understand* it.

To get you to the best start possible I want to list here the reasons why OPM is the world's most powerful fortune builder. Then I'll be certain you understand and sense the glory of OPM. Once I know this I'll be 99 percent convinced that I can make *you* rich. Some wealth builders call the magic of OPM the world's greatest money secret. Here is that secret.

The World's Greatest Money Secret

OPM works like magic because it:

- Lets you concentrate on building an enormous income
- Frees you of constant money worries
- Stimulates you to greater efforts
- Gets important money people interested in your business
- Opens a regular source of cash to you
- Builds a solid credit rating for you
- Triples your wealth-building speed
- Quadruples your self-confidence
- Puts you on a jet-propelled path to riches

Read these nine magic keys over and over again. Paste them on a card that easily fits into your wallet or purse. Memorize these magic secrets until you can repeat them by heart. Why? Because the more familiar you are with the world's greatest money secrets, the easier it will be for you to find, obtain, and use OPM!

Put the World's Greatest Secret to Work

An engineer friend of mine in New Orleans, Louisiana, couldn't stand the 9-to-5 routine of his job. Thinking things over he decided he had to make a pile of money as quickly as possible. We talked over his problem during one of my business trips to Louisiana.

"Paul," I said, "right now you're in an ideal mental state to start earning big money in your own business. When a person is dissatisfied with his present life he's willing to take risks. Have you thought over what you'd like to do?"

"Yes," he said. "I'd like to speculate in land—right near here," he continued, naming an area in a nearby state.

I let out a whistle. "That area is probably the worst place in the world for land speculation today, Paul," I said. "Land isn't selling too well there. Yet just because that area has such a reputation at this time doesn't mean you'll fail. In fact, with so few people speculating in land there at this time, you just might be able to make a go of it."

"That's exactly what I've been thinking," he said with a grin. "But I need some money to get started. If I could borrow three thousand dollars I could make a down payment on an ideal industrial property."

"Paul, I think you need something else before you start trying to borrow any money," I said.

"What's that?" he asked eagerly.

"The nine keys to the world's greatest secret."

Paul frowned. "What are they?"

"Here, I'll make a list for you." I then wrote out the list exactly as I have given it.

Paul studied the list. "It seems to make some sense," he said. "But it doesn't put any money in my pocket."

"It will, soon enough," I said.

"How?"

"Just memorize the list and I'll show you how."

Paul spent the evening memorizing the list. While he was doing that I checked on the availability of money in New Orleans. Most of the banks, I learned, had cash reserves that were readily available for business and personal loans.

When we met the next morning I had Paul repeat the nine keys for me. He remembered every one perfectly.

"Now I want you to apply for a loan at that bank," I said to Paul, and pointed across the street. "As you go into the bank, repeat the nine keys to yourself. If the interview seems to be going badly, pause a moment and repeat as many of the keys as you can. Then continue the discussion—and come out with the loan approved!"

Getting Money Using the Secret

Paul strode into the bank while I waited outside. Twenty minutes passed before he burst out of the door, grinning delightedly.

"They approved the loan," he shouted. "I'm on my way to a fortune!" He shook my hand so excitedly that I almost lost two fingers.

"Tell me about it over a cup of coffee." I laughed. "But first give me my hand back."

"It was easy," Paul said as we sipped our coffee. "I did just as you told me. I just kept repeating the keys as the loan officer asked me questions. I was so confident that the keys would work that the loan officer was calling me 'Sir' within three minutes after I sat down in his office. When I told him how much I needed he said, 'You can borrow twice that much, if you wish, Sir.'"

Paul borrowed the three thousand dollars and made the down payment on the industrial property. Within six months he sold it for a profit of four times his down payment. Recently he called me from New Orleans to say that he was ready to retire for life at the ripe age of 29. "I made nearly two million dollars in two years," he said happily. "And it all resulted from the nine keys and OPM. Thanks a million, pal."

Thinking over Paul's call I told myself that his experience was typical of the results any of my friends or readers could expect when they used the world's greatest money secret. Further, if Paul could make almost two million dollars in two years in an area where land was not in great demand, then in areas of rapid land turnover my readers would earn a million dollars in less than one year using OPM.

How the Secret Works

The world's greatest money secret works in several different ways. These ways are:

(1) You start your search for OPM fully confident that you'll get it.

(2) Your confidence radiates to the lender—he is so sure of you that he *wants* to lend you money.

(3) The success of negotiating the loan gives you the drive to plunge ahead to an enormous income.

(4) As each loan and its associated business or investment succeeds, you build up a stronger drive to achieve great wealth.

(5) Nothing succeeds like success, except more success. You succeed in one deal after another, creating an unbeatable skill to earn a larger and larger income.

"But," you say, "I'm not as young as I used to be. My strength and enthusiasm aren't what they were ten years ago."

"Forget it," I say. "Once you have the money from that first loan in your hand your enthusiasm will double. And, surprisingly, so will your strength and stamina. A burning desire to earn big money can often improve your outlook on life—and your health.

Bob B., a civil-service worker in the post office, spent years dreaming about buying his own business. But his post-office salary was so small that Bob couldn't think of borrowing money to start a business until his kids grew up. To make matters worse, within a week after his last child left home, Bob was sick in bed.

"Bob," I said to him as I stood by his bedside, "you have to get better so you can start the business you've always dreamed of."

His eyes lit up. "Gee," he said, "I hadn't thought of that. All I've been doing while I lie here is think of how sick I feel."

"Stop thinking of yourself and start thinking of being successful," I told him. "You know, Bob, you *might* just get better and you *might* make some extra money."

Bob started planning his business moves. Soon he began to get well, partly, I believe, because he was planning for the future and he forgot the little aches and pains almost everyone has. Soon after he left his sick bed Bob applied for and obtained the business loan he needed. Within a year he was able to resign his post-office job to concentrate on his own business.

Use Your Success Power

Over the years I've advised and watched hundreds of fortune builders like Bob B. Their success has led me to a number of conclusions about beginning wealth builders. The most important of these findings is this:

As a beginning wealth builder you have an enormous success power hidden within you. Once you release this power you have a giant positive force which pushes you straight towards your wealth goal.

I've watched hundreds of men and women in the grip of success power. Many of these people know almost nothing about business, law, taxes, etc. Yet they are driven from poverty to wealth by the enormous force of success power which grows out of the magic of OPM.

While you're gripped by success power you:

- Seldom make serious mistakes
- Gladly take business risks
- Have greater belief in yourself
- Seek, and find, the best way to make money
- Make friends quickly and easily
- See situations clearly, accurately
- Get to the real core of problems
- Feel that nothing can stop you
- Plunge ahead with super energy
- Function smoothly—both mentally and physically

Many people I've observed know very little about the technical facts of the business they've chosen. Yet while they're in the grip of the success power generated by OPM, they rocket ahead to great wealth. Some people, like Sam T., begin with $400 of borrowed money and build it to half a million dollars in three years. How did Sam T. build wealth so quickly?

Putting OPM to Work for You

Sam T. invested his borrowed money in valuable postage stamps. While investing, Sam joined several stamp clubs. He told the club members that he was investing in really valuable stamps. Naturally the club members wanted to see the stamps. Sam showed them to the members and soon had several offers to buy the stamps at prices higher than he paid for them. Sam sold the stamps to the club members and reinvested his money in other valuable stamps. Soon Sam had a list of people who wanted to buy his stamps as he acquired them.

Why could Sam sell his stamps at a profit? There are several reasons. (1) Sam studied the field and learned which were the desirable stamps. (2) He interested the club members in these stamps by telling them stories about the history of each valuable stamp. (3) Sam: (a) located the important stamps, (b) purchased the stamps, (c) displayed the stamps, and (d) prepared, and sold, with each stamp, a history of the stamp. Thus, Sam provided a valuable service to the club members. For this service Sam deserved, and received, a fair profit.

Sam's big break came when several large, wealthy stamp clubs asked him to sell to their members. He provided them with so many excellent stamps that his services and stamps were eagerly sought by other clubs. Three years after he started, Sam was worth half a million dollars.

Just Ask for OPM—and Learn

"I'm not too interested in OPM right now," you say. "What I'm more interested in is learning the ins and outs of the business world."

"Fine," I say. "One of the best ways to learn about the business world is to go out and try to borrow some money. You'll learn a great deal in a hurry."

Why? Because when you ask for OPM you quickly learn the important questions people have about existing and new businesses. Typical questions you may be asked are:

(1) What is the actual or potential profit of the business?

(2) What are the actual expenses of the business?

(3) How many employees do you need in the business?

(4) How long has the business been showing a profit?

(5) What is the ratio of fixed expenses (rent, heat, light, etc.) to variable expenses (materials, productive labor, etc.)?

(6) For what purpose will the borrowed money be used?

(7) How long will it take to repay the loan you are seeking?

Learning Pays Off

A little learning is a dangerous thing—particularly in business. This is exactly what Ben T. learned when he tried to borrow some money to use to buy a restaurant.

Ben knows the kitchen end of the restaurant business—in fact, Ben's veal cutlets are the best I've ever tasted anywhere. But being the world's best cook doesn't make a man a successful restaurant operator. Ben learned this when he was interviewed at a bank where he applied for his loan.

"What profit do you expect from this restaurant?" the banker asked.

Ben frowned. "Oh, about five hundred dollars a week," Ben answered.

"What percentage is that?"

Ben sputtered. "I don't really know."

"But you have to know the answer to that and a lot of other questions before I can approve a business loan for you," the banker said, in a distinctly annoyed tone.

Ben was in very low spirits when he left the bank. His chances of owning his own restaurant seemed to have disappeared forever. It was shortly after his disappointing bank interview that Ben and I met at a business reception.

We began talking about borrowing money and that's when Ben told me his sad tale about bankers and bank loans. As Ben talked I spotted his trouble—he was "heavy on the well-done side but light on the meat." By that I mean that Ben knew the techniques of restaurant cooking operations backwards and forwards. But the dollars and cents aspects—the meat of the business—was lacking from Ben's skills list.

Convert a No to a Yes

"Ben," I laughed, "you look worried. But I don't think your problem is that serious."

"Well, I'm glad to hear you say that," Ben said with a touch of doubt in his voice. But just how do I convince a bank that I'm a good credit risk?"

"There's only one way I can see right now, Ben. You have to get yourself a business manager—a guy who may not know peanuts about gravy but who does know what a profit and loss statement is."

"How can I find such a person?" Ben wailed. "All my friends are in the kitchen end of the business."

"Advertise in your local paper, Ben. Or put an ad on the bulletin board of the local men's club. Just think of several ways to get in touch with people and I'm sure you'll find the person you want.

"Further, Ben, you're a valuable property. Keep that in mind!"

"Me a valuable property? How do you figure that?"

"Easily, Ben. Look—you're a top-notch cook who wants to open his own place. Your cooking is so good that I know you'll be a big success. Your ability will help a businessman get a loan which a bank might not make if you weren't in business with him. Also, your tie-in with the businessman makes it easier for the bank to grant the loan because both of you, if necessary, can sign the loan application. And remember, Ben, one of the main reasons a bank is in business is to *make* loans. A bank doesn't earn a profit when it refuses a loan—it just wastes time and *loses* money!"

Ben advertised for a business partner and was swamped with offers. "What do I do now?" Ben asked plaintively about a week later.

"Pick your business partner as carefully as you chose your wife, Ben," I said. "With the right business partner the sky is your limit. But with the wrong partner you could go broke in three months. I've seen too many people go wrong with a poorly chosen partner."

Pick Business Partners Carefully

Ben spent several weeks interviewing the businessmen who had expressed interest in his project. He made his choice but hinged his final acceptance of the partner on approval by a bank of a loan application for enough money to open the first restaurant.

Together Ben and his partner prepared a financial statement and description of the business. They went to the bank together and came away with a $50,000 five-year loan in less than 30 minutes! Today Ben and his partner have five booming restaurants and more income than they know what to do with. And all of their success is based on OPM which came as a result of business learning paying off.

Now Let's Borrow the OPM

Are you convinced that OPM is the answer for your business or investment needs? I hope you are because I am determined to show you, step by step, exactly where and how to borrow the money you need for any business or investment that interests you.

Further, I'll show you how to put the borrowed money to work to earn the highest profit it can. I want you to earn the largest amount of money possible in the shortest time. The way to accomplish this goal is by use of OPM. So let's get started right now with the easiest kind of OPM for most people to obtain—the personal loan.

During our journey through the world of OPM we'll also show you:

- Where to get lists of hundreds of lenders
- How to go into your own overseas business for $48
- Where to get 2,500 business leads for $25
- Ways to earn big finder's fees
- How to make real-estate deals that bring you millions
- Valuable publications to help build your wealth
- How to become an insider; i.e., a financial broker
- Plus many other wealth-laden tips

Use a Personal Loan as Your Springboard to Riches

An important key to successful borrowing of OPM is knowing what kinds of loans are available in your area of the country. I usually summarize this important rule by telling new wealth seekers:

Always make it a practice to know who's lending money for what purposes in your area.

Why? Because when you know who's lending, and for what purposes, you can plan your approach much better. This improves your chances of having your loan application approved.

Personal Loans Are Easy to Obtain

Many beginning wealth builders think that they must have a *business* loan for business purposes. This is not so!

Suppose you borrow $5,000 using a personal loan. Isn't that $5,000 the same amount of money as $5,000 borrowed on a business loan?

"Yes," you answer, "but what about the interest? Wouldn't the interest be much higher on the personal loan? Why pay higher interest rates?"

These are excellent questions and they show that you're really alert. Now fellow fortune builders, I want you to listen to your good friend, the author of this book. I've made a pile of money using OPM so I know what I'm talking about. This is what I say:

When you're first starting your fortune hunt, interest on OPM is unimportant; what is important is that you obtain the OPM!

When you borrow from a bank or other licensed lender the interest you pay is not excessive. Further,

If you invest OPM so it only earns the interest you pay, you're in the wrong business and you'd better get out before you go broke!

Also, I want you to remember this key fact about OPM: *Interest you pay on OPM is easily proven and it is a legally deductible item on your income tax return.*

So while a personal loan *may* cost you a *few* dollars more in interest payments than a business loan, the extra cost is insignificant. What *does* matter to you and to me in our fortune-building efforts is this:

Personal loans are the easiest and fastest kinds of loans for the beginning fortune builder to obtain. Hence, they are worth concentrating on until a business or investment program is solidly established.

When you're starting a business, expanding a going firm, or getting an investment program underway, you usually have many more items on your mind than money. So if you can get the money you need in a hurry you can push ahead quickly and earn more. Since a personal loan will give you the money you need in a short time—usually within four to twenty-four hours after you apply for the loan—you should carefully consider applying for a personal loan the next time you need money for business.

Where to Obtain Personal Loans

Check the ads in your largest local newspapers. You may find one or more banks advertising personal loans.

Don't be led astray by thinking that banks advertising auto and mortgage loans are out of the personal loan business. Read the ads carefully. Near the bottom of the ad you may see a line or paragraph saying: "Do you need a personal loan? Come see us. Our Personal Loan Department makes personal loans on your signature for amounts up to $5,000 and periods to 36 months."

Check the *Yellow Pages* of your telephone book. Most banks and finance companies making personal loans will have ads in this handy reference. Call the banks or finance companies and ask them to send you data on their personal loans. With the loan papers available in the privacy of your own home, you can take all the time you need to study the loan charges (if any), interest rates, repayment periods, etc. While studying the loan papers, note this important fact:

To obtain a personal loan you need no collateral at all. The money is lent to you on your signature—all you need do is sign the loan application after giving certain information about yourself.

Check other loan sources in your area to learn if they make personal loans. Typical personal loan sources other than banks and finance companies are religious organizations, business firms, financial brokers, insurance companies, financial advisers, and close friends. But your best source today probably is your local bank or finance company.

To obtain a monthly comprehensive listing of the newest important loan sources of all types, subscribe to *International Wealth Success*. This monthly newsletter lists many capital sources from which you might be able to obtain a personal or business loan, if you qualify. The newsletter also contains many other money-making wealth items such as finder's fees, international business opportunities, mail-order leads, export-import needs, etc. To subscribe to this helpful newsletter for one year, send $24 to International Wealth Success Inc., P.O. Box 186, Merrick, N.Y. 11566.

How to Qualify for a Personal Loan

Banks and finance companies are in business to earn money from the interest they charge on the loans they make to you. When a bank or finance company lends you money the organization wants to be as certain as it can that you will *(a)* repay your loan on time, *(b)* use the money for constructive purposes, and *(c)* continue to do business with the bank or finance company. To ensure itself that you will meet these objectives, every bank and finance company has certain qualifying standards for personal loans.

The qualifying standards you must meet vary somewhat from one bank to another, and one finance company to another. But, in general, to qualify for a personal loan of $1,000 or more you must:

(1) Have a steady job or own a business
(2) Have worked for one organization for six months or more
(3) Have lived at the same address for six months or more
(4) Have a telephone in your home
(5) Own an automobile or some other personal property

Can you see what the bank is seeking when it sets up these loan standards? The bank is trying to establish a pattern of living for you. Thus, the bank believes that:

- If you're a steady worker now, you'll continue to be one in the future
- If you've lived in one place for a while you'll probably continue to live there
- If you have a telephone you've established some dependability
- Owning an automobile or other valuable personal property shows that you've accomplished something in life

Knowing that such loan standards exist puts you way ahead when you apply for a loan. Why? Because you know which aspects of your job or business background to emphasize when you talk to the loan officer. Also, if you apply for a loan and you're turned down, you can figure out why, if the lender refuses to tell you why.

Check Your Borrowing Power

Banks and other lenders, like most other businesses today, are busy The loan officers, whose job is to approve or disapprove your loan application, are rushed. They don't always have as much time as they need or would like to have to study your application and financial situation.

To save time in evaluating loan applications, some banks and lenders use a *point system*. Here, for the first time in a book written for the general public, is a complete and concise review of the point system. You can use this review to check your borrowing power while you expand your know-how about this important applicant rating technique.

Rate Yourself Now

Most point systems are set up to include the following items: your age, marital status, telephone ownership, number of dependents, residence data (own or rent), time on your job, type of work you do, wife's occupation (or husband's), weekly income, monthly income, annual income, monthly installment payments you are now making, and your credit history on other loans or installment plans.

Recently a *streamlined point system* has become popular. It covers just six items—time on the job, weekly income, property ownership, credit rating on previous loans, time at one rental address, and ability to make a down payment on an article that will be bought.

Let's take an example of a loan application and rate it with each system; i.e., the (a) comprehensive method, and (b) quick method.

Then, knowing your own financial situation, you can quickly rate yourself using either or both methods.

A Typical Personal Loan

Our loan applicant is Mr. BWB—Mr. Beginning Wealth Builder. He has worked as an auto mechanic in a local garage for two years where he earns $150 per week. Mr. BWB is 35, married, with two children. His wife works part time in a local shop. The family lives in an unfurnished rented apartment which they have occupied for the last two years. They have their own phone. Mr. BWB has paid off several loans in the past and has a good credit rating, though at times there has been some slowness in his repayment of loans. At the present time he is making monthly installment payments of $175 on a car. Now let's rate Mr. BWB, using the Point Score System shown in Figure 2-1.

MR. BWB's POINT SCORE

Item	Score	Item	Score
Age	0	Employment	0
Marital Status	+1	Wife employed	+1
Phone	0	Weekly income	+3
No. of dependents	0	Monthly income	+3
Residence	0	Annual income	+3
Job time	+1	Installment payments	−2
		Credit rating	−2

Adding up Mr. BWB's score we find that it is +8. According to the instructions for Figure 2-1, Mr. BWB's loan can be approved on the spot by the loan officer.

How to Score Yourself

Let's take a quick look at each item in the Point Score System of Figure 2-1 to see how you score the item, using the data for Mr. BWB. To save space we'll refer to Mr. BWB as *he*.

Age: He's 35; hence he is rated 0.
Marital status: He's married so he's rated 1.
Phone: He has a phone so he's rated 0.
No. of dependents: He has two children and a wife, or a total of 3. Since this is under 5, he's rated 0.

POINT SCORE SYSTEM

		Over 70 Disqualify	All Others 0			SCORE
AGE	Under 25 −1					
MARITAL STATUS	Divorced & Separated −2	Single 0	Married +1			
PHONE	No −2	Yes 0				
NUMBER OF DEPENDENTS	Under 5 0	6-7 −1	Over 7 −2			
RESIDENCE	Owner Over 5 yrs. +4	Owner 0-5 yrs. +2	Rent less than 1 yr. −1	Rent 1-5 yrs. 0	Rent Over 5 yrs. +2	
TIME ON JOB	Less than 1 yr. −1	1-3 yrs. +1	4-10 yrs. +2	Over 10 yrs. +4		
TYPE OF EMPLOYMENT	Attendant, Barber, Bartender, Cook, Domestic	Cab Driver, Hospital Orderly, House Painter	Laundry Laborer, Musician, Porter	Nurse Aide, Practical Nurse, Waitress	Window Cleaner, Self Employed All: −3	
WIFE EMPLOYED	Yes +1	No 0				
INCOME (WEEKLY)	Less than $75 0	$75-$100 +1	$100-$125 +2	Over $125 +3		
INCOME (MONTHLY)	Less than $325 0	$325-$433 +1	$433-$542 +2	Over $542 +3		
INCOME (ANNUALLY)	Less than $3800 0	$3800-$5200 +1	$5200-$6500 +2	Over $6500 +3		
MONTHLY INSTALLMENT PAYMENTS	$0-$50 +2	$50-$100 +1	$100-$160 +1	Over $160 −2		
CREDIT BACKGROUND	Bankruptcy-repo.-judg. Disqualify	Serious deling. −4	Some Slowness −2	No Record 0	Satisfactory +3	

APPROVED _____ DECLINED _____ BY _____   TOTAL _____

- If total score is +8 or more, the application can be approved without review with credit manager.
- If total score is +3 or less, the application can be rejected without review with credit manager.
- If total score falls within the range of +4 to +7, review application with credit manager.

Courtesy of The Credit Union Executive

Figure 2-1: Point score guide

Residence: Since he has rented for the last two years he is rated 0.

Job time: He's been on his job 2 years so he's rated +1.

Employment type: He's not one of the listed types so he's rated 0.

Wife employed: His wife works so he's rated +1.

Weekly income: Since he earns $150 per week he's rated +3; i.e., over $125.

Monthly income: To find his monthly income, multiply the weekly income by 4 1/3. Since it is over $542, he's rated +3.

Annual income: Multiply the weekly income by 52. Since this is over $6,500, he's rated +3.

Monthly installment payments: He is paying $175 a month on a car; hence he is rated −2.

Credit background: He has a past history of some slowness in his payments; hence he is rated −2.

JOB TIME		WEEKLY EARNINGS	
Under 1 year	0 points	Up to $75	0 points
More than 1 year but under 5 years	10 points	$76 to $100	15 points
Five to 10 years	15 points	More than $100	20 points
More than 10 years	25 points	Wife has earnings	5 points

PROPERTY OWNERSHIP		CREDIT RATING	
Owns property with little or undetermined cash value	10 points	No previous credit history	0 points
Owns property for 5 yrs. or longer, or cash value is twice loan amount	20 points	Good (with a bank)	25 points
		Good (other)	10 points
		Good record with this lender (bonus points)	10 points
Property owned free and clear	30 points	Poor	−10 points

HOME OR APARTMENT RENTAL HISTORY		DEPOSIT ON PURCHASE	
		Up to 10 percent deposit	0 points
Under 1 year	−10 points	10 to 35 percent deposit	10 points
1 to 5 years	0 points	More than 35 percent deposit	20 points
More than 5 years	10 points		

Figure 2-2: Simplified point score system

Add the ratings, taking the sum of all the plus ratings, or +12. Do the same for the minus ratings, or −4. The sum of these two is +8. As the instructions at the bottom of Figure 2-1 indicate, a score of +8 or more means that the application can be approved on the spot by the loan officer.

Try the Simplified System

This quick system uses points, Figure 2-2, for just six items. A score of 60 points is required for approval of a loan application.

Applying this system to Mr. BWB's loan application we find the following:

Time on job: His 2 years rate 10 points
Weekly income: A weekly salary of $150 rates 20 points
Wife's income: Since his wife works, add 5 points
Property ownership: He doesn't own property; 0 points
Credit rating: Favorable (bank); 25 points
Rental history: Two years rates 0 points
Down payment: Ignore because this is not an appliance loan
Total Points: 60

Since Mr. BWB has a score of 60 points his loan application would be approved on the spot by the loan officer.

When checking yourself with either of these point systems keep this important fact in mind:

Banks and other lenders carefully indicate that any point system is merely a guide for the loan officer. There are numerous loans made to people whose score is lowered by unusual circumstances.

So if you fail to pass either point system, cheer up! There's still plenty of hope that you'll still get the loan you need.

Another Point System

Here's a third point system you can use to check your loan application eligibility. It is a copyrighted Scoring System owned by Field Promotions Inc. and is the prime Scoring System used in banks today for loan applications and credit cards. In this system, Figure 2-3, you

Courtesy of Field Promotions, Inc.

Figure 2-3: Bank point score system

	AGE					A
A	21-25 1	26-35 2	36-45 2	46-64 2	65 & OVER 1	

	MARITAL STATUS					B
B	SINGLE 1	SEPARATED 1	DIVORCED 1	WIDOWED 1	MARRIED 2	

	DEPENDENTS (INCLUDING YOURSELF)					C
C	ONE 2	TWO 2	THREE 2	FOUR 1	FIVE OR MORE 1	

	LIVING FACILITIES					D
D	WITH PARENTS 1	RENT: FURN. 1	RENT: UNFURN. 2	OWN-MTG. 4	OWN NO MTG. 5	

	YEARS AT PRESENT ADDRESS					E
E	UNDER 1 YR. 1	1-2 YRS. 1	3-5 YRS. 1	6-10 YRS. 2	OVER 10 YRS. 2	

	YEARS AT PREVIOUS ADDRESS					F
F	UNDER 1 YR. 1	1-2 YRS. 1	3-5 YRS. 1	6-10 YRS. 2	OVER 10 YRS. 2	

	TOTAL MONTHLY INCOME					G
G	UNDER $400 1	$400-600 1	$601-800 3	$801-1000 5	OVER 1000 7	

	YEARS WITH PRESENT EMPLOYER					H
H	UNDER 1 YR. 1	1-3 YRS. 2	4-6 YRS. 3	7-10 YRS. 4	OVER 10 YRS. 5	

	TOTAL MONTHLY OBLIGATIONS (INCLUDING RENT OR MTG. PMT.)					I
I	UNDER $75 2	$75-125 1	$126-200 2	$201-300 1	OVER $300 1	

	OCCUPATION					J
J	HOME WORKER-OTHER 1	BLUE COLLAR 2	SKILLED OR EQUIV. 3	EXEC. OR SUPER. 4	PROFESSIONAL 4	

1

Circle the number on each line that describes you and write it in the code box to the right.

2

Add your scores plus bonus points. Enter your total score.

3

If you have scored 17 points or more complete the additional information, seal and mail today

BONUS POINTS

ADD 2 POINTS IF YOU HAVE A TELEPHONE LISTED IN YOUR NAME

ADD 5 POINTS IF YOU HAVE ANY LOAN EXPERIENCE AT THIS BANK

ADD 3 POINTS FOR LOAN EXPERIENCE AT OTHER BANK OR FINANCE CO.

ADD 2 POINTS IF YOU HAVE A CHECKING OR SAVINGS ACCT. AT THIS BANK

REMINDER: *IF YOU SCORE 17 POINTS OR MORE MAIL TODAY!* **TOTAL SCORE**

THE RIGHT OF FINAL LOAN APPROVAL IS RESERVED BY THIS BANK

just pick out your rating on each of the lines A through J. You get bonus points; i.e., extra points, for each of the four items listed at the bottom of Figure 2-3. Note that you receive seven points if you've done business with the bank in the past. The "winning" score for this system is 17 points.

Mr. BWB discussed in the example above would get the following points in this system, assuming he does *not* do business at this bank:

A.	Age: 2	F.	Years at previous address: 1
B.	Marital status: 2	G.	Total monthly income: 5
C.	Dependents: 1	H.	Years with present employer: 2
D.	Living facilities: 2	I.	Total monthly obligations: 1
E.	Years at present address: 1	J.	Occupation: 3

Thus, Mr. BWB would score 20 points without taking advantage of the bonus points. (In rating him, I assumed that he had lived two years at his previous address, that his wife earns $200 per month, and that his total monthly obligations are over $300). Since Mr. BWB scored 20 points, and the passing grade is only 17 points, his loan would be quickly approved.

"Sell Yourself" to the Lender

Whenever you apply for a personal loan, keep this important fact in mind:

Loan officers are human; they want your business. "Sell yourself" to the loan officer and you have a much better chance of having your loan application approved.

To "sell yourself" effectively, check the following before, during, and after each personal loan application you make:

Appearance—Are you neatly dressed in business clothes?

Appointment—Do you arrive at the lender's office on time?

Application—Have you filled out your loan application as neatly as possible?

Politeness—Are you as polite as you can be to the loan officer even when he is not enthusiastic about your loan?

Purpose—Do you have a good purpose for needing the loan?

Pay Period—Are you ready to agree with the loan officer on the repayment period he recommends?

Have a Good Purpose for Your Loan

For what purposes do banks and other lenders make personal loans? There are hundreds of purposes but the most popular and the most quickly approved purposes for personal loans are to pay for:

Medical expenses	Educational expenses
Furniture	Dental work
Vacation	Auto or home repairs
Funeral expenses	Emergency expenses

"But," you say, "I want a *business* loan. I'm not interested in borrowing money for a vacation!"

"Certainly," I reply. "But if you follow a typical Mr. BWB around you'll soon see that every time he applies for a business loan he's turned down because he doesn't have a business yet. Now I'm not saying that you have, or will have the same borrowing troubles Mr. BWB has. But just in case you do, or one of your friends does, the borrowing purposes listed above will be most useful."

"But how does borrowing for a vacation, or for any of the other reasons you've listed above help me?" you ask.

"Here's how. Let's say you borrow $5,000 for three years. Your payments will be $160 per month for 36 months. You plan to spend most of the money on a European vacation. But after you receive the check from the bank you change your mind and decide to invest the money in a business. Should you run back to the bank to return the money? No!" Why? Because:

Once a bank makes a loan for a given period, the officials don't want overly early repayment. The bank makes money when you take the full term to repay the loan.

Use Dual Purposes

Does it disturb you to change your mind after you've applied for a loan? I know some people who feel guilty if they borrow for one purpose and later decide to use the money for another purpose. If you're this type of person, then I have a great idea for you:

Use dual purposes when applying for your personal loan. Then you can use the money for either purpose without feeling guilty.

But here's an important word of caution. When applying for a personal loan, be sure to emphasize the personal aspects of the loan; that is, any of the reasons listed above. Why? Well, if you emphasize the business aspects of your loan, the loan officer might say "What you really need is a business loan. I recommend that you see our man in the commercial loan department."

This can give you problems because the requirements for a business loan are much stricter than for a personal loan. If you doubt what I say, simply apply for each type of loan and see what the results are.

Dream Up Your Own Purposes

Suppose that instead of using one of my suggested purposes for borrowing money on a personal loan, you decide to use one of your own purposes. Fine! The more creative you are, the greater your potential success in your own business.

But I hope you're not like the BWB who tried to borrow $5,000 for three years to pay income taxes. The bank turned him down instantly. Why? Because banks and other lenders refuse to lend money for more than a year for purposes that recur annually—such as income taxes. Had this BWB taken my advice he could have easily obtained the money he needed. So while I want you to be creative, I also want you to put my hints to work. Try them and see. They'll really work for you!

Don't Lose Your Cool

Don't allow unnecessary guilt about the purpose of a loan stand in your way to becoming wealthy. When you borrow money to use in a business you are being creative. You are putting OPM to work and, hopefully, you will make the OPM grow. When this happens, you benefit from the profits earned, the bank benefits from the interest it receives on the loan, and the people with whom you spend the borrowed money benefit.

Creative use of OPM is your key to building a fortune today. Without smart, aggressive use of OPM it is almost impossible to build a large fortune in the present economy.

Take Larry M., a clerk in a stockbroker's office. Larry never earned enough to invest in the stock market. Also, though he was interested in 19th century American paintings, he never had enough money to buy those he wanted.

One day Larry discovered several Frederic Church paintings in a small art gallery. Larry felt that the prices of these paintings were almost certain to increase as more people discovered the great beauty and talent displayed by the artists working in America in the 1800's. So Larry resolved to buy some of the paintings, using a $5,000 personal loan. He hoped that the paintings would increase enough in value to enable him to show a profit on their sale. Until he sold the paintings, Larry planned to use a portion of his regular income to make the monthly payment on the loan.

Larry talked to the gallery owner and learned that business was far from booming. Since Larry felt that the Church paintings were certain to increase in value, he made a deal with the owner. For $5,000 cash the owner would sell Larry two of the paintings and reserve three others for him. The cost of the three reserved paintings would be $3,000 each, when Larry was ready to buy them.

It took Larry three years to pay off his $5,000 loan with monthly payments of $160. But before two years had passed, Larry was offered $15,000 *each* for the five paintings. Larry waited another year and sold all the paintings for $100,000—that is $20,000 each!

Since the total cost of his loan was $5,760, and the three reserved paintings cost $9,000, Larry's total cost was $14,760. His gross profit was therefore $100,000 − $14,760 = $85,240 in three years! Averaging this over three years, Larry's annual gross profit was $85,240/3 = $28,413.33. This is a neat annual gross profit—particularly when you remember that Larry didn't invest a dime of his own—he earned all this on OPM, by visiting galleries during his spare time. You can do the same if you invest wisely.

Give Yourself a $100,000-a-Year Raise

Larry spent three years to net about $85,000. He's delighted with the results of OPM. But Claude L. is a man in a hurry. When I told him about Larry, Claude shrugged his shoulders. "I don't have three years to wait," Claude said a trifle testily. "I want to hit it big the first year. If I go out and borrow money I want a big payoff for my time and for the risks I take!" Claude said this during a consulting conference I had with him on my boat.

"Claude, I know of one way you can go from zero income to an income of $100,000 per year on borrowed money. If you call that a big payoff, then you can have it."

"Now you're talking my kind of money," Claude laughed. "Tell me how I can get this $100,000-per-year income on OPM," Claude said, his eyes gleaming.

"You have to pyramid loans, Claude, *after*—and only after—you find the right kind of an investment to make."

"Pyramid loans," Claude asked in a puzzled voice. "What's that?"

"Let's find an investment first. Then I'll show you."

Privately I had decided to have Claude invest in rental real estate. I told him this and we both began watching the real estate ads in the local newspapers, trying to find suitable rental property. Further, I contacted several real-estate brokers and told them what Claude was seeking—a large net income from rental property with a small down payment.

Two weeks later Claude called me. I could tell he had found something because there was excitement in his voice. "I've got it," he shouted. "Listen to this." As he read the ad I visualized it. Here's the ad as it ran in the paper:

> $30,000 per year net income on a cash investment of $30,000. Ten apartment houses, 200 units. Profit can be increased. *Write* Box 100.

Claude wrote immediately. A few days later I helped him inspect the ten buildings. While they needed work, they were basically sound and actually earned the profit the owner claimed.

Pyramid Your Way to Wealth

Here's what I had Claude do to obtain the $30,000 OPM he needed to take over the buildings:

(1) Inquire about a $5,000 personal loan at six *different* banks.

(2) Obtain a loan application from *each* bank while discussing the loan.

(3) Fill out *each* loan application.

(4) On the *same* day, drop off the loan application at each of the six banks.

(5) Deposit the six loan checks in a checking account in one bank.

(6) Make the down payment on the buildings.

The Loan Pyramid at Work

Now let's see how this works in dollars and cents. Claude's monthly net profit from the buildings is $30,000/12 = $2,500. His monthly payment on the six personal loans is 6($160) = $960. Hence, his net spend-able *money in the fist* (MIF) is $2,500 — $960 = $1,540 per month. And, after three years, his MIF = $2,500 per month.

"What," you ask, "pays the other bills—the fuel, repairs, and most important of all, the mortgage on the buildings?"

The income from the property pays all these bills and Claude's profit. The 200 units have an average rental income of $1,000 per year; i.e., the average rent per apartment is $83.33 per month. With 200 units the gross annual income is 200 ($1,000 per unit per year) = $200,000. With a profit of $30,000 per year, the money left to pay for fuel, repairs, *and* the mortgage is $200,000 — $30,000 = $170,000.

Claude took over the property, as I advised, using the loan pyramid-ing technique. He soon found that his actual profit was nearly $40,000 per year, instead of the estimated $30,000.

Using these buildings as the core of his fortune-building program, Claude took over two more groups of buildings that year. His net in-come, as of December 31st, topped $100,000 per year.

Here Are Answers to Your Wealth Questions

Every time I tell someone about this personal-loan pyramiding tech-nique a number of questions arise if the person I'm talking to is un-familiar with the way a bank operates. Here are the most important questions that are asked, along with their answers.

Q. Won't one bank check with another to see if I've applied for a loan?

A. No! The bank wants you as *its* customer. Banks check with each other *only* when (a) you fail to make a payment on your loan, (b) you give the name of another bank as a reference, or (c) you tell one bank that you have a loan at another bank when you apply for a second loan. If you follow my technique there is very little chance that one bank will check with another, unless you ask that this be done. (And there's seldom any need to *ask* the bank to check with another bank.)

Q. Won't the bank check out my credit rating at a central credit bureau?

A. Yes, if there's any question about your credit. But if you've paid off all your loans (for cars, appliances, etc.) the bank may not bother to make a credit check. The important concept to keep in mind is that the approval of your loan application hinges on (a) the impression you make on the loan officer, (b) the points you score on the credit scale, as shown earlier in this chapter, and (c) your previous credit history.

Q. Won't the bank turn down my loan application because I've applied for loans at more than one bank?

A. No! The bank may not check with the other banks. Do you think bank A wants bank B to know that you're thinking of becoming their customer by taking out a loan? Many people seem to think that banks are secretly trying to check up on them. This isn't so! Banks want you as their customer, not as their enemy.

Q. Do I have to lie to pyramid loans?

A. No, not if you apply for a loan at each bank on the *same* day. Then it will be true when you state in your application that you have no other loans outstanding. Keep another important fact in mind:

Just as it is completely legal for you to shop around in many stores for the best buy in a new coat, so too is it completely legal for you to apply at several banks for the best deal on a loan you need.

Say Goodbye to Fear

Rid yourself, here and now, of two wealth-inhibiting attitudes that kill more loan applications than any other. These attitudes are:

(a) Fear of banks, bankers, or their documents. Bankers are human—just like you and me! They *want* your business. So stop being afraid of banks, bankers, and their documents. The fact that a man does business in a marble hall doesn't make him any better than you are!

(b) Believing that banks never make mistakes. Banks are run by bankers who are human beings. Since almost everyone makes a mistake now and then, bankers, being human beings, also make mistakes. Thus, a bank may turn down your loan application in the mistaken belief that you don't earn enough to repay the loan. Or you may receive 37 payment coupons in a 36-payment loan book. Or you may deposit $3,000 in the bank and receive credit for only $2,000!

So banks do make mistakes, just like everyone else. Starting here and now, rid yourself of a fear of bankers and their systems. Keep a careful eye on everything your banker does. Double-check his arithmetic—sooner or later you'll catch him in a mistake. Then politely ball him out. You'll feel better after you do and your banker will have more respect for you.

Know What Your Loan Will Cost

Experienced wealth builders often refer to the borrowing of money as the *renting* of money. Just as another person might rent an apart-

ment for a year, these wealth builders rent $5,000, $100,000, or $1,-
000,000 from the bank for a month, a year, or several years. The "rent"
they and you pay is the interest charge on your loan. And like other
business rent, your interest payments are tax deductible from any profits
you earn.

You wouldn't rent an apartment without knowing the monthly or
annual rental charge. So too with a loan—you should know how much
a loan will cost you before you take it out. Further, since I want to
make you a sophisticated money borrower, I recommend shopping
around for loans to learn what each lender charges. This shopping will
give you poise and confidence. You'll soon be able to look any banker
or lender in the eye without a bit of fear.

Large companies shop around to get the cheapest rent (i.e., interest)
possible on their loans. So why shouldn't you?

Here Are Actual Loan Costs

To give you an idea of the typical costs of personal loans I've assembled data from several banks and states and listed the costs in the
table that follows. (Not all states allow you to borrow the same amount
on just your signature.) The repayments listed do *not* include life insurance on your life during the period of the loan. While the cost of
life insurance varies with the amount of money you borrow, if you add
$1.00 per month to the loan repayments listed, you won't be far off.

COST OF PERSONAL LOANS

Amount you repay monthly

Amount you receive	12 mo.	24 mo.	36 mo.	60 mo.
$5,000	437.44	230.20	161.97	109.29
4,500	393.70	207.18	145.77	98.36
4,000	349.96	184.16	129.58	87.43
3,500	306.21	161.14	113.38	76.50
3,000	262.70	138.12	97.02	65.66
2,500	218.72	115.10	80.99	54.65
2,000	174.98	92.08	64.79	43.72
1,500	131.23	69.06	48.59	32.79
1,000	87.49	46.04	32.39	21.86
500	43.74	23.02	16.20	10.93

I recommend that you use a 36-month repayment period because my experience shows this is best for Mr. BWB. Also, you can always pay off your loan sooner—if you earn enough profit from your business. Note that the total cost of the loan = what you repay in 36 months minus the cash you get. If you pay off your loan in less than 36 months the total cost of the loan will be less than shown in the table.

Borrow Money by Mail Order

Do you find loan interviews difficult? Are you embarrassed when you go to the Loan Department of a bank? If the answer to either question is yes, don't feel guilty. Many people have similar feelings. When I meet these people I usually recommend that they take out a personal loan by mail order.

"I never heard of such a thing as a mail-order loan," most people exclaim. "But that's just the kind of a loan I need. How do I go about getting one?"

You have to know which banks and lenders make mail-order loans. Without this information you're lost, because only a small percentage of banks and other lenders are willing to make such loans. While you can conduct a long and time-consuming research program to find the names of banks and other lenders willing to make mail-order loans, there is a shorter way.

Subscribe to the monthly newsletter *International Wealth Success.* This idea-laden newsletter lists many sources of mail-order loans which I'm certain you'll find helpful. To begin your one-year subscription to the newsletter, send $24 to International Wealth Success Inc., P. O. Box 186, Merrick, N. Y. 11566. You'll quickly learn that the IWS newsletter contains hundreds and hundreds of other unusual and useful wealth-building ideas.

Get Reliable Loan Data

"There's only one bank in my town," you say. "And that bank has turned down my loan application six times. What do I do now?"

You must get *reliable* loan data. The mere fact that one bank or lender turned you down doesn't mean the next one will—if you know which banks and lenders are looking for borrowers. One of the best ways I know of to obtain the names and addresses of banks and lenders ready to lend money is to subscribe to the monthly newsletter *International Wealth Success,* mentioned above.

This newsletter contains lists of Capital Sources every month, as well as Finder's Fees, International Profit Opportunities, Profitable Business Ventures, etc. Some of the Capital Sources listed offer 100 percent financing for real estate deals, company mergers and acquisitions, etc. One item in one issue could help you build an enormous fortune on OPM in a few years.

Build Your Credit Rating

Every year thousands of beginning wealth builders (BWBs) hit the big money by using OPM. Many of these BWBs have no credit rating of any kind when they start their search for wealth using OPM. Yet they hit the big money. How—without a good credit rating? Let's see.

If you don't have a credit rating of any kind, or your credit rating is poor because of difficulty in paying off a previous loan, you have to take a series of positive steps to build your personal credit rating. Here, for the first time in print, is my success-laden method for quickly establishing your personal credit rating.

Three Easy Steps to a Great New Credit Rating

Follow these three steps and you'll quickly improve your credit rating.

(1) *Establish a permanent residence address.* Let's say your job or family situation has forced you to jump around the country for the last several years. When you apply for a loan the quick changes in residence don't look good on your application. Every bank likes to think that if they have to give you a ring on the phone some day, you'll be at your present address, and not in some other state. What can you do?

Check your relatives and friends. Do you know any long-time residents of the local area with whom you've lived or stayed? Will any of these people be willing to allow you to use their address as your residence for the past several years? If so, your application will probably be accepted much faster. Any other technique you can develop to establish a legitimate permanent address will have much the same effect.

(2) *Build a record of steady employment.* People run into employment problems on loan applications when they have changed jobs frequently. Once again, a bank likes to believe that you are a steady, reliable worker who is kept on the payroll by a company. And the larger the company, the better your chances for approval of the loan application.

Suppose you've hopped around from job to job. What can you do? Did you have a business of your own during the years you were job-hopping? Were you thinking of forming your own business during that time? If you can establish a steady record of working for yourself in your spare time—even though you had only very small profits, or no profits at all—your application will have a much better chance of being accepted. And, incidentally, you need not tell the bank that your business earned very low or no profits.

To use a spare-time business as an aid in obtaining a loan, be sure you:

(a) Have a business name
(b) Use a business address
(c) Sell, or try to sell, a product or service
(d) Have plans for future sales increases
(e) Have a business card and letterhead

(3) *Raise your income statistics.* The higher your income, the larger the personal loan you can obtain—up to the limit in your state ($5,000 in some states; $7,500 in other states). Thus, the man earning $15,000 a year can borrow more than the man earning $5,000 per year. But how can *you* increase your income statistics? Here are several ways.

(a) Include your spouse's income, if you're married. Two incomes are better than one!
(b) Add all your other income to your job income. Include interest, dividends, loan repayments to you, etc. Remember—the higher your income, the higher your loan.
(c) Find other income sources you can call your own. Thus, if a relative or friend will assign his income to you, your income will be higher.

Smart Personal Loans Build Wealth

You *can* get rich using the magic of OPM obtained through personal loans. Put the wealth-studded tips in this chapter to work and you can soon be richer than you ever thought possible. Using my techniques you might:

• Build a $200,000 service business in six months starting with a $5,000 personal loan
• Take over $300,000 worth of real estate using three $5,000 personal loans
• Earn an annual profit of 150 percent on every dollar you borrow.

There are hundreds of other profitable deals you can set up using OPM obtained from personal loans. You'll learn about these as you read further in this book. Meanwhile, check your local area for the availability of personal loans. You'll find that there's more money waiting for you than most people realize.

How to Get
Instant Personal Loans

All through Chapter 2 we assumed that the credit rating of every reader was nearly perfect, or could easily be made nearly perfect. So the borrowing methods I gave you in that chapter are the more conventional ones; that is, they allow you to get a personal loan quickly and with little fuss.

The Real World of Borrowing

But few lives are completely perfect—particularly in the real world of OPM—other people's money. How do I know? I know from daily experience because for many years I've approved—or disapproved—daily loan applications made to a million-dollar-per-year lending organization. Yes, good readers, among my many other activities, I am the elected president and chief loan officer in a highly reputable financial organization!

So you are reading the words of the man who sits on the other side of the desk—the bank's side—when you apply for your loan. Over the years I've heard almost every story a borrower can tell. Some of these stories are extremely convincing—others wouldn't be believed by a five-year-old.

In this chapter I want to show you how to present such an effective personal loan application that any bank or lender will instantly approve your loan. If you have a great credit rating, stop reading here and skip to Chapter 4. But if you're just a trifle doubtful about your credit rating, then read on. This chapter *is* for you.

What You Need for Instant Approval

Every lender—be it a bank, finance company, insurance company, or a commercial factor—wants to be as certain as possible that when it makes a loan:

(1) The loan will be repaid in full
(2) Every payment will be made on time
(3) No chasing of the borrower will be necessary
(4) The money is used for acceptable purposes

The only way the lender can ensure that these needs are met is by insisting that the borrower meet certain credit requirements. When the borrower doesn't meet the credit requirements on his own, the lender may insist that further security be provided. This chapter shows you many different ways to provide that security.

Use a Cosigner to Build Your Credit

Let's say the lender turns down your personal loan application. You ask him why you were refused. "Insufficient income," he replies.
"If I get a cosigner, will you approve my application?"
"Yes, if the cosigner's income is high enough."
"What do you mean by that?" you ask.
"Well, his income should be enough to enable him to pay off the loan in case you can't." You scratch your head and go away to think things over.

A Million-Dollar Secret

Now let me tell you a secret about most lenders. Your cosigner's earnings are scrutinized a lot less carefully than your earnings because:

Having a cosigner makes it much easier to obtain any personal loan. Lenders feel far safer with two signatures on a loan application.

When you have a cosigner (also called a comaker) you'll often see a cold, unfriendly loan official change to a warm, friendly, willing-to-lend pal. Just the fact that someone is ready to cosign on a loan for you makes you more attractive to the lender. This sounds silly, I know, but this is the way life works in the *real* world of borrowed money.

Who Can Be a Cosigner for You?

You can have relatives and friends, or both, as cosigners. Why do I use the plural in the above sentence? Because some lenders may want more than one cosigner. Or you may decide to pyramid cosigners; that is, use two or more cosigners whose ability to pay adds up to the required amount.

Typical acceptable cosigners include:

Brother	Cousin
Sister	Aunt
Father	Uncle
Mother	Friends

Note that your wife (or hubsand) is not in the list. The reason for this is that some banks will ask that your spouse cosign on every personal loan, regardless of whether you have another cosigner. Hence, you can't depend on using your spouse as a cosigner with every lender. But those lenders who don't require the spouse to cosign *will* gladly accept the spouse as your cosigner.

Relatives are a good source of cosigners, if you don't object to their learning a great deal about your financial situation.

When you ask relatives to cosign a loan for you be prepared for a *yes* and then a *no*. Why? Because some of your relatives will decline to cosign when they learn what information they must supply the lender. This information may include:

Employer's name	Other income
Length of employment	Debts owed
Monthly or weekly earnings	Property owned
Marital status	Home and business addresses

Where possible, ask only one close relative (mother, father, brother, sister) to cosign on a personal loan. This approach leaves any other relatives available for cosigning of future loans—should you need such a loan.

Sometimes the relatives in a happy, closely-knit family are ready to cosign on any loan. In your exuberance to get started on building your fortune you may offer a number of cosigners' signatures to the lender. Take my advice:

Supply the exact number of cosigners the lender requests—but no more. Supplying more than the needed number of cosigners doesn't improve your chances for obtaining the loan, but it may prevent you from using the extra cosigners on a future loan.

Lenders aren't impressed by large families. But they are impressed when you can come up with a suitable cosigner earning the required amount to cover the loan.

Some Friends Are Better Than Relatives

Many beginning wealth builders strongly object to using relatives as cosigners on personal loans. "I haven't seen my relatives in years," they say. "Besides which, they couldn't care less about what I do."

If this applies to you, then think about asking some of your friends to cosign for you. Carefully consider,

(a) Do I have any *really* close friends?
(b) Would any of these friends cosign for me?
(c) Are the cosigner's earnings high enough?
(d) Am I resentful over giving friends financial details?

Almost all of us, at some time during our lives, have one or more friends who are close enough to us to become cosigners on personal loans. Hold onto such friends; they're valuable! Having a good friend when you need one could make the difference between earning a fortune on OPM, and not earning a fortune. So be nice to everyone; you never know when you'll need a cosigner for a loan!

Paying a Cosigner Can Be Worthwhile

"But," you say "I don't have any friends, my relatives are scattered all over the country, and the bank demands a cosigner. What do I do?"

You can *pay* someone to be your cosigner. It's done every day.

"But isn't that dishonest?" you ask.

No; it isn't! Furthermore, there isn't a single dishonest tactic recommended in this book. Some of the financial tactics recommended are shrewd; some are creative; others were secret, until this book was written; lastly, certain of the tactics are so original in concept and require such a dedication to put into action that only a sincere BWB would use them. But the tactics are *here*, in this book, ready for your use. *And they're all honest and legal!*

Is it dishonest to pay a blood donor whose donation of blood saves your life? No, the best of people use blood donors when they need them. Likewise, it isn't dishonest to pay someone to cosign a loan for you, *provided* your cosigner will repay the loan in the event you cannot.

Where do you find cosigners who are available for a fee? Here's how.

Spread the word among your friends and acquaintances that you have heard of someone who's willing to pay a fee for cosigning a loan. Do not identify the person needing the loan. People react more favorably when they don't know who needs the cosigner. Remember this:

In becoming a cosigner a person accepts full responsibility for the loan. Hence, you may have to "sell" a person to become a cosigner.

While "selling" a person to become a cosigner may seem difficult, it is usually easier to do this than it is to "sell" a bank on your ability to pay off a loan without a cosigner, after the bank has requested a cosigner.

How Much Should You Pay a Cosigner?

As little as possible! Some hungry cosigners may accept 1 percent of your loan—i.e. $50 on a $5,000 loan. Others may insist on 2, 3, 4, or 5 percent of your cash proceeds from the loan.

Don't, unless you are in great need of a personal loan for *business* purposes, pay the cosigner more than 5 percent of your cash proceeds. This means you would pay the cosigner $250 on a $5,000 loan.

Try Offering a Finder's Fee

Large and small companies seeking business loans often offer a *finder's fee* to anyone finding a lender willing to make a suitable loan. You can do the same. To get the best results from the finder's fee you pay:

Make cosigning the loan a part of the finder's fee requirement. Then you get double results—a loan source and a cosigner—from the same fee.

How much should you pay a finder? Avoid paying more than 5 percent of the cash you receive. The cosigning portion of the fee—say 3 percent—is *part* of the 5 percent.

Here's a further interesting aspect of using a finder's fee:

Many people become enthusiastic about earning a finder's fee and arranging for the cosigning of a loan. But if they are approached only for cosigning they refuse to participate in the loan.

What does this mean to you? Simply this—people will do what you want (cosign) when they're earning a finder's fee. But they're much less likely to do what you want (cosign) when they're being paid only to cosign.

Why is this? What is there to a finder's fee that is so powerful? I've analyzed this many times and concluded that a finder's fee has a romantic attraction to most people. They derive a hidden joy from being a *finder*. To obtain this hidden joy most people are willing to do a little more; i.e., cosign on the loan.

Advertise for Finders

Study the classified columns of your newspaper and you'll see plenty of ads for capital wanted. But you'll find hardly any ads for finder's fees. Why? Because most people and firms paying finder's fees advertise in exclusive and specialized financial publications. You can do the same, and get the loan you need.

International Wealth Success runs finder's fee ads free of charge for its regular annual subscribers. Since the annual subscription fee is a nominal $24, you gain in two ways by reading this interesting newsletter:

(1) You see many finder's fee ads.

(2) You can run your own finder's fee ads free.

Use Ready-Reserve Plans

Banks in recent years have become more understanding about borrowers than ever before. Why? One word explains it all—*competition*. The smaller, more alert banks throughout the country are continually trying to woo customers away from the large banks. To do this the small banks offer many tempting services to their depositors. One of them—*ready reserve*—is also offered by the large banks.

Ready reserve works like this. You apply for a ready reserve of a certain amount—say $5,000. The application you fill out for ready reserve is similar to an application for a personal loan. In fact, when approving a ready reserve of a certain amount, a bank is actually granting you a personal loan for that amount. The difference is that most people don't take or use their ready reserve immediately—instead they wait until they need the money.

Once your ready reserve application is approved the bank sets aside the amount covered—in this case $5,000. Then, if you write a check that exceeds the amount of money you have in your checking account, the bank uses money from your ready reserve to pay the check. Thus, you can write a check for up to $5,000 above the amount you have in your checking account because your ready reserve covers it.

Why do I recommend reserve to you? There are several reasons:

- Ready reserve is often easier to obtain than a personal loan
- Ready reserve teaches you to manage and invest your money more carefully
- Ready reserve can quickly put you on the road to great wealth

How to Qualify for Ready Reserve

To qualify for ready reserve you have to, in general, meet the following:

(a) You must have, or must open, a checking account in the bank granting the ready reserve.

(b) You must intend to maintain a checking account in the bank until any amount advanced you on your ready reserve account is paid back.

Paying Off Ready Reserve Loans

The usual charge for ready reserve funds is 1 percent per month of the unpaid balance. Thus, if you use $1,000 of your ready reserve, you pay the bank 0.01 ($1,000) = $10 per month until you have repaid the $1,000, or reduced it by repaying all or a portion of it.

Now let's say you owe the bank this $1,000 for two months and you then repay $200, reducing your ready reserve to $800. The monthly charge will then drop to 0.01 ($800)=$8.

Some banks have an arrangement whereby a stated amount is withdrawn each month from your checking account to pay off a portion of your ready reserve loan. Or you can specify, if you wish, how much should be deducted from your account to pay off the loan. Banks usually allow you up to one year to pay off small loans of $1,000 or less. Up to three years is allowed for larger loans.

Other Types of Personal Credit

The banks in your area may offer different versions of ready reserve. Thus, some banks have *executive credit* plans; others have *checking account backup* plans. Most of these plans are similar in intent to ready reserve. The important idea to keep in mind is that these plans can furnish you with instant cash for your business activities.

One key feature of ready reserve type plans that is often overlooked is this:

You are seldom asked the purpose of the loan for ready reserve because the bank knows that it is difficult for you to predict in advance the use you'll make of the money.

Since some BWB's have difficulty determining the purpose of their loans, the ready reserve solves this problem. Also, as we said earlier, it is usually easier for you to get a ready reserve type loan.

Keep Up to Date on Loans

Banks keep dreaming up new kinds of personal loans. Why? Because:

Banks and other lenders are in business to lend money to you. The more ways they can develop to lend you money, the more loans they make.

Read your local newspaper and watch for loan ads. Study the *Yellow Pages* of your phone book under the headings of *Banks, Loans, Finance.* If you want the names and addresses of banks, insurance companies, financial brokers, and other lenders throughout the United States and other parts of the world interested in lending amounts up to several million dollars, subscribe to *International Wealth Success,* which will supply you with hundreds of leads each year on sources of personal loans.

Typical *new* personal loans offered by bankers and others are the:

> Back-to-school loan
> Brighten-your-kitchen loan
> Fix-up-the attic loan
> Executive vacation loan
> Check-guarantee-card loan
> Home-remodeling loan

These personal loans, and many similar personal loans, are easier to obtain than other types of loans. Why? Because when a bank or finance company introduces a new type of loan, the officials are interested in granting as many of these new loans as possible. The bank wants to show as much new-business activity as it can. So the bank will approve your loan faster and more easily. Keep this fact in mind when you are looking for instant personal loans.

Build Up to Big Personal Loans

Banks and finance companies love people who pay off their loans on time. You can build on this known characteristic of lenders and profit from it. Here's how:

Borrow a small amount—say $500—and pay it back quickly. When, on the basis of your record, the bank offers to lend you more, accept the offer and take a larger loan.

Some BWBs find it difficult to believe that banks are looking for people who will borrow money. But if these people could sit in on a few bank loan department conferences they'd soon realize that many banks are crying for customers to whom they can lend money. I'll prove this to you right now!

Here's the Proof You Want

To prove how interested banks are in making new loans to proven customers, I'll show you two letters from excellent banks. After you read these letters we'll comment on them.

Dear Mr. _____

You are paying off your loan in excellent fashion. We enjoy doing business with you. Further, your regular payments on your loan have established your credit with us. Should you need more money —even before your present loan is paid off—stop by to see us.

If you don't have time to visit us, call _____ and talk to our Loan Officer. He will be delighted to help you obtain the funds you need. Should you prefer to do business by mail, just fill in and send us the enclosed short form. We'll mail your check within a few days.

Remember—you can renew your loan, if you wish. By renewing your loan now you can obtain the money you need—and the payment terms best suited for you—quickly. If you wish, you can wait three months before you start making payments on certain types of loans.

You can borrow from us at low, low rates for personal reasons, for a new or used car, for a boat, for a vacation, for home improvements—in fact, for any *good* reason.

So if you need extra funds, please stop by. We want to do business with you!

• • • •

Dear Friend:

We were delighted to serve you this year through our Loan Office, and we were highly pleased with the way you repaid your loan. Your fine record established your credit at the Bank of_____. We'd like to serve you in the future whenever you need money.

Do you need funds for home improvements, a new car, a home appliance? We'd be delighted to talk to you about a low-cost loan fitted exactly to *your* needs.

Please give us a ring any time the Bank of _____ can serve you. No matter what your financial needs may be, you'll find we're happy to help you. Just dial us at _____, or stop in to see us. You'll find a friendly welcome whenever you come in.

Make the Best of Your Chances

Let's analyze these letters. But before doing so I want you to note that:

(a) Both these banks are among the finest in the world.

(b) The two banks have widely different backgrounds—No. 1 is primarily a business bank; No. 2 is mostly a personal bank.

(c) These two banks are in different parts of the country.

Yet these two banks—as different in their background as man and woman—have the same objective: *they want to lend you more money because you were so reliable when paying off your first loan!* You proved your dependability. And banks love dependable customers!

Note in the first letter that "you can renew your loan, if you wish . . ."
And, ". . . to do business by mail, just fill in and send us the enclosed
short form. We'll mail your check within a few days." Also, "You can
borrow from us at low, low rates . . ." Lastly, "We want to do business
with you." Note that you can get your second loan with this bank by
mail order!

In the second letter, note that "Your fine record established your
credit at the Bank of _____. We'd like to serve you in the
future whenever you need money." Also, "No matter what your financial
needs may be, you'll find we're happy to help you."

I could show you hundreds of other letters like these which prove
that banks like to do business with their proven customers. Knowing
this, you can easily begin to build your fortune using OPM.

Easy Figuring of Interest Rates

Many BWBs worry excessively about the annual rate of interest—
for example, 5 percent, 6 percent, 7 percent, etc.—they pay on their
loans. While you should know exactly how much each loan costs you,
I'd rather see you worry about how you'll make a profit on your borrowed money. To reduce the worries about interest costs that some
BWBs have, an easy and quick way to figure annual interest rates is
given in Figure 3-1. Let's see how you can use it.

ANNUAL RATES

When the lender states that his finance or carrying charges are based
only on the unpaid balance or amount of money still owed, figure your
annual interest rate from:

Stated finance charge per month on unpaid balance	Annual rate, %
½ of 1%	6
¾ of 1%	9
5/6 of 1%	10
1%	12
1¼%	15
1½%	18
2%	24
2½%	30
3%	36

Figure 3-1

When your finance or carrying charges are based on the *beginning amount owed and are included* in 12 equal monthly installments, the annual rate is shown in Figure 3-2.

12 EQUAL MONTHLY PAYMENTS

Quoted finance charges	Annual rate, %
$ 4 per $100 or 4% per year	7.3
$ 6 per $100 or 6% per year	10.9
$ 8 per $100 or 8% per year	14.5
$10 per $100 or 10% per year	18.0

Figure 3-2

THE RULE OF 78

Suppose you've just borrowed some money from a bank and you're sitting in the loan officer's office. "Here, Mr. BWB," he says, "is your check for $4,000. We're delighted to do business with you," he continues, and shakes your hand.

You accept the check, after glancing at the amount shown on it. Then you have a sudden thought about repaying the loan. "Would I save anything if I paid this loan off early," you ask.

"Certainly," the loan officer replies. You just use the *rule of 78* to figure your rebate."

Now you may have heard of the rule of 78, and you may not have. For those who haven't, here's a quick rundown on it.

Let's say you borrow $2,400 for 12 months and that the total finance charge (excluding life insurance) is $156. To use this rule, add the number of each month for the borrowing period. For a 12-month loan, add $1+2+3+4+5+6+7+8+9+10+11+12=78$.

Now the rule of 78 says that the finance charge that must be paid each month is the number of months remaining for the loan be paid off, divided by the sum of the months as found above. Let's see how this works for your loan (Figure 3-3).

Now let's say you want to pay off your loan at the end of the fifth month. What would your finance charge be? How much would you save in finance charges by paying off your loan at the end of the fifth month instead of the twelfth month?

To find the finance charges for five months, simply add the month's finance charges for the first five months in the table above, or $24 + 22 + 20 + 18 + 16 = 100. Thus, you'll save $156 - 100 = $56 in

Month No.	Months to go	Month's finance charge
1	12	$(12/78) \times \$156 = \$\ 24$
2	11	$(11/78) \times\ 156 =\ 22$
3	10	$(10/78) \times\ 156 =\ 20$
4	9	$(\ 9/78) \times\ 156 =\ 18$
5	8	$(\ 8/78) \times\ 156 =\ 16$
6	7	$(\ 7/78) \times\ 156 =\ 14$
7	6	$(\ 6/78) \times\ 156 =\ 12$
8	5	$(\ 5/78) \times\ 156 =\ 10$
9	4	$(\ 4/78) \times\ 156 =\ 8$
10	3	$(\ 3/78) \times\ 156 =\ 6$
11	2	$(\ 2/78) \times\ 156 =\ 4$
12	1	$(\ 1/78) \times\ 156 =\ 2$
		Total $= \overline{\$156}$

Figure 3-3

finance charges by paying off your loan at the end of the fifth month instead of the end of the twelfth month.

You can use this procedure for a loan of any size to which the rule of 78 applies. Note how your monthly finance charge decreases as time goes on.

RATE FOR DISCOUNTED LOANS

The usual personal loan which a bank makes to you is made quickly and easily. You go into the bank, fill out the application, talk to the loan officer a few minutes, and then go away. A few hours later the phone rings and the loan officer says "Mr. BWB, your money is ready." You go to the bank and pick up your check. About two weeks later you receive a book of coupons which are used when you make your monthly payments on your loan.

There is no talk of the rule of 78 or any other item we've mentioned thus far. But the loan officer may mention that "Your loan will cost you $4.75 per hundred per year discounted." Now what does he mean by this?

He means that for every $100 you borrow for one year the bank subtracts (i.e., *discounts*) $4.75 in interest in advance. So you receive only $100.00—4.75 = $95.25 for every $100 you borrow. On the $2,400 loan we mentioned above, your discount or interest cost is ($2,400/$100) ($4.75) = $114. So you would receive $2,400 — 114 = $2,286 in cash, but you would repay on the basis of having received $2,400. When considering a discount type of loan, imagine yourself receiving the full amount in cash and then immediately paying the banker his interest from the money you receive. What you'd have left is the cash you actually receive. (Other discounts charged per $100 are $5.25, $6.50, $7.25, $7.50, etc.)

If your loan is more than one year—say for two years—the amount deducted in advance is 2x$4.75 = $9.50; for three years it is 3x$4.75 = $14.15 per $100 borrowed. To find your interest or finance charge in dollars per hundred, just multiply the discount per hundred dollars by the number of years for which you'll hold the money. Find your total cost by multiplying the above amount by the number of hundreds of dollars you plan to borrow. Now let's find the *rate of interest* you pay on discounted personal loans.

Useful Interest Table

To help you figure quickly the interest rate on any kind of loan, a simple, useful interest-rate table is included in this chapter (Figure 3-4). Here's how to use this table in five easy steps.

(1) Determine the total amount of money you will finance, i.e. borrow.
(2) Figure the finance charge.
(3) Select the number of months for repayment.
(4) Divide the finance charge, item (2) by the total amount financed, item (1). Multiply the result by 100.
(5) Enter the accompanying interest table at the number of months for repayment and project to the finance charge. At the top of the column read the interest rate.

Let's apply these steps to the $2,400 loan mentioned above which runs for 12 months at $4.75 per $100, discounted. The total amount to be financed, item (1), is $2,400. The finance charge, as we figured it above, is $114. Then, for Step 4, ($114/$2,400) ($100) = $4.75. Entering the table at 12 months and projecting horizontally to $4.75 we find that this amount lies between $4.66 and $5.22. Following the column between these two numbers vertically upwards, we read the approximate annual interest rate as 9 percent.

When using this table, note that the annual interest rate is approximately the rate appearing at the top of the two columns between which the finance charge per $100 falls. If the finance charge per hundred falls exactly on a listed value, the lower percentage rate can be used.

APPROXIMATE ANNUAL INTEREST RATES

(Finance charge per $100 of balance financed)

No. of level monthly Payments	5%	5½%	6%	6½%	7%	7½%	8%	9%	10%	11%	12%	13%	14%
6	1.39	1.54	1.68	1.83	1.98	2.13	2.27	2.49	2.79	3.08	3.38	3.68	3.97
12	2.59	2.87	3.14	3.42	3.69	3.97	4.25	4.66	5.22	5.78	6.34	6.90	7.46
18	3.80	4.21	4.61	5.02	5.43	5.84	6.25	6.86	7.69	8.52	9.35	10.19	11.03
24	5.02	5.56	6.10	6.64	7.18	7.73	8.27	9.09	10.19	11.30	12.42	13.54	14.66
30	6.25	6.92	7.60	8.28	8.96	9.64	10.32	11.35	12.74	14.13	15.54	16.95	18.38
36	7.49	8.30	9.11	9.93	10.75	11.57	12.40	13.64	15.32	17.01	18.71	20.43	22.17
48	10.00	11.09	12.18	13.28	14.39	15.50	16.62	18.31	20.59	22.90	25.23	27.58	29.97
60	12.54	13.92	15.30	16.70	18.10	19.52	20.94	23.10	26.01	28.96	31.96	34.99	38.06

No. of level monthly Payments	14%	15%	16%	18%	20%	22%	24%	26%	28%	30%	33%	36%	
6	3.97	4.27	4.57	5.02	5.61	6.21	6.81	7.42	8.02	8.63	9.39	10.30	11.22
12	7.46	8.03	8.59	9.45	10.59	11.74	12.89	14.05	15.22	16.40	17.87	19.66	21.46
18	11.03	11.87	12.72	13.99	15.71	17.44	19.19	20.95	22.72	24.51	26.76	29.50	32.26
24	14.66	15.80	16.94	18.66	20.98	23.33	25.70	28.09	30.51	32.96	36.05	39.81	43.63
30	18.38	19.81	21.26	23.45	26.40	29.39	32.42	35.49	38.60	41.75	45.73	50.60	55.54
36	22.17	23.92	25.68	28.35	31.96	35.63	39.35	43.14	46.97	50.86	55.80	61.83	67.98
48	29.97	32.37	34.81	38.50	43.52	48.64	53.85	59.15	64.56	70.05	77.04	85.61	94.38
60	38.06	41.17	44.32	49.12	55.64	62.32	69.14	76.11	83.21	90.45	99.68	110.03	122.64

Figure 3-4

Instant Money Can Be Yours

Follow the hints in this chapter and you can have your personal loan approved within a few hours—maybe even a few minutes. Why wait days and days when, by using the right techniques, you can have your money in less than a day?

I want you to get as rich as possible as soon as possible. And the first step in the process of getting you rich is to have you obtain your starting capital easily and quickly. Should you need more money than you can obtain through a personal loan—and most businessmen eventually do—just read on to learn how you can put other valuable tech niques to work building a great fortune for yourself.

4

You Can Obtain
Profitable Business Loans

When you borrow money for personal reasons—such as for medical expenses, a vacation, school tuition, etc.—you use a *personal loan*. The true interest costs on a personal loan are usually a little higher than on any other kind of loan. Why? Because there usually is a greater risk for the lender when he makes a personal loan. So interest, as we saw earlier, is charged on a *discounted* basis on many personal loans.

Business Loans Can Help You

Business loans are made on the basis of *simple interest*. Thus, if your loan is at 6 percent simple interest, you pay 0.06 ($100) = $6 per year for every $100 you borrow. Stated another way, you pay 6 cents per year for every dollar you borrow. Thus, you will pay $60 interest per year for every $1,000 you borrow.

"Why then," you ask, "should I ever think of taking out a personal loan when a business loan is figured on the basis of simple interest? Earlier, as I recall, you said that personal loans are figured on a discounted basis. To find the approximate true simple interest on such a loan, you double the stated interest rate. This gives a true interest rate of eleven percent in my areal So tell me why I should *ever* take out a personal loan?"

There's just one answer to this question. To every BWB this answer is highly important. The answer is:

To obtain a business loan you must, in general, own a going business. If you don't own a business, your chances of obtaining a business loan are slim.

This is why many BWBs turn to the personal loan for their *first* financing. Once they've established their business they then take out business loans.

Advantages of Business Loans

There are four big advantages that business loans offer you. These are:

- Lower interest cost
- Less frequent payments
- Easier renewal of the loan
- More favored treatment by bank

Let's take a look at each of these advantages.

Lower interest means that you have more money left for profit. But this advantage really doesn't become a major factor until you have loans of $100,000, or more.

Less frequent payments can really be a help. Thus, some banks and other lenders will allow you to pay on your loan once a year. This makes your business life simpler, compared with making monthly payments on your loan. When a bank allows annual payments, you are often required to pay the interest in advance. But the interest cost is small compared to the amount you borrow—the *principal*. You can arrange to have the interest deducted from the principal, or you can pay it out of the principal.

Easier renewal of your loan can be a big help. Let's say you borrow $10,000 for a one-year period. At the end of the year you find that you'd be better off if you waited a few months before you repay the $10,000. So you *renew* your loan; i.e., you extend it for another year. To do this you just sign a new note with the bank and pay the interest for the next year. Interest on a $10,000 loan at 6 percent simple interest would be $600.

More favored treatment by the bank makes you feel good. It's nice to be an "in" customer. But what is much more important is that you can get your money faster when you need it. This could mean the difference between a fast closing on a deal and losing out on the deal.

How to Get into a Going Business

Note that lenders make business loans to *going businesses*. But not every going business is a *profitable* business. So you can have your own unprofitable going business and still be eligible for a business loan. Silly, isn't it? But that's the way it works. Now let's see how you can put yourself into a going business.

Let's say you want to start your own direct-mail and mail-order business. This is a dream you've had for as long as you can remember. But like many BWBs you need capital to get started and you don't have the capital. Without an established business, your business loan application will probably be turned down. Here's an answer that might work for you.

(1) Establish a business—register the name in your town or state.

(2) Pick a business address—your home address is good enough for now.

(3) Get a telephone number—again, your home phone can be used at the start.

(4) Have business letterheads printed at a local print shop.

These four items will cost you less than $25 in most states. "Why should I spend $25 without any assurance that I'll get it back?" you ask, after some thought.

Because your $25 investment (which you'll eventually have to make if you go into business) may enable you to obtain a $5,000 business loan. Isn't it worth spending $25 to get a loan that can put you on the road to wealth?

Let's say that you take these four steps and establish your mail-order business. What do you do next? The answer is simple—you make business plans.

Ways to Plan Your Business

Sit down with a piece of paper and a pencil. Ask yourself:

How much income can I generate for each dollar I spend in this business at the start? One year from now? Two years from now?

Write down your answers. In the mail-order business you should be able to generate at least $3 in sales for every $1 you spend to get new business. So if you obtain a $5,000 business loan and spend all of it, after suitable testing, on obtaining new business, you will generate gross sales of 3($5,000) = $15,000.

Now, what profit might you expect on such a sale? Much depends on the cost of your product and your overhead (rent, light, heat, labor, etc.) expense. I personally know many mail-order operators who earn a 35 percent profit because they manufacture their products in their own home. Other mail-order men earn a 10 percent profit because they pay a high price for their products and operate out of a plush office Let's say you plan to operate carefully and expect to earn a 20 percent profit. This is a completely reasonable assumption.

So, with gross sales of $15,000, your profit will be 0.20($15,000) = $3,000. This is nearly the amount you want to borrow–$5,000. Should your profit rise to 35 percent, as it easily could, you have a profit of 0.35($15,000) = $5,250, or *more* than you borrowed!

Tell the Lender Your Story

When we say that you earn 20 percent profit we mean that you have 20 cents of every income dollar available after you pay *all* the expenses related to your business. One of these expenses is the salary you receive for the work you do. As a BWB you will probably be willing to reinvest some of your earnings in the business.

To be more certain you obtain every business loan you apply for, tell the lender:

(1) You will earn a high profit
(2) You will use both the profits and some of your earnings to pay off the loan
(3) Your profit prediction is based on sound business facts–not guesses
(4) Your whole fortune is tied up in the business; you'll work hard to make the business go.

Trying to obtain a business loan when you're just starting a business isn't easy. But it can be done. Here's how one BWB got the business money he needed.

Test Your Way to Wealth

Pete R. wanted to start a mail-order business. But he lacked the capital and every lender he contacted said: "Prove to me you can make a 20 percent profit before taxes and I'll lend you the money you need."

Note that these lenders weren't asking for a certain profit in dollars –just a profit percentage. Thus, a $20 profit on $100 worth of sales gives you the same profit percentage as a $2,000 profit on $10,000 in sales. This points up an important principle–

The profit percentage you expect in a business is extremely important when you're negotiating a loan. So be sure you know the profit you can earn in your business.

Pete R. couldn't start a full-fledged mail-order operation because he didn't have enough capital. But he did have $100 to spend to test 1,000 names on a suitable mailing list. Pete prepared his sales letter and flyer carefully. To create a better impression and increase the response, Pete used first-class mail.

Sixty-three people ordered products from this mailing. This is a response of 63/1,000 = 0.063, or 6.3 percent—an excellent percentage. On this sale Pete showed a profit of 32 percent.

Taking his figures to the lender, Pete quickly obtained the loan he needed. Testing is necessary in every well-run mail-order or direct-mail business. When you can make testing help you obtain the capital you need, you're getting double value for your money—that is, (1) sales, and (2) facts that will convince a lender that you have a bright future

Try Short-Term Business Loans

An important borrowing principle you should keep in mind at all times is this:

The longer the term of your loan, the more cautious the lender becomes. For this reason, you may find it easier to obtain a short-term loan.

What is a short-term loan? Any loan made for less than a year is a short-term loan. Typical short-term loans run for 60, 90, 120, 150, 180, 210, 240, 270, or 300 days.

How do you obtain a short-term loan? By filling out an application that resembles a personal loan application. You present this application to the loan officer and he approves it after you sign a short-term loan note. But instead of receiving a check, the lender usually transfers the amount you borrow to your checking account. This brings up another important point:

If you borrow money for business purposes from a bank, your loan has a much better chance of approval if you have your business and personal checking accounts at the bank.

This makes sense—a bank likes to do business with its regular customers. While you don't have to maintain your checking accounts at the bank granting you short-term business loans, you'll find your loan application is approved much faster if you do.

How Short-Term Loans Can Help You

Let's say you borrow $10,000 for sixty days to purchase some products you've already sold. This is a technique used by thousands of businessmen all over the world.

You deliver the products to your customers and send each a bill. Half your customers pay within sixty days—the other half are slow payers and you must wait a little longer before you receive your money. "But," you ask with a worried expression, "what about my $10,000 loan? Will the bank get the sheriff after me?"

No, the bank won't! You needn't worry about that. Since you've received half the money you owe the bank, you have several alternatives open to you:

(1) Pay off half your loan and *renew* the note for another sixty days for half the original amount.

(2) *Renew* the note for 60 days for the full amount you owe.

(3) *Pay off less* than half the note—say 20 or 30 percent—and *renew* the note for the balance.

Thus, a short-term loan doesn't have to be repaid when it comes due. All you need do is *renew* the loan; i.e., sign a new promissory note *and* pay the interest—usually in advance. Plenty of businessmen use this technique of renewing the note to keep loans for years. But remember one important fact about renewing your short-term loans:

Banks and other lenders insist that you pay the interest on every short-term loan. So you must earn at least the interest from your investment.

Now let's take a quick look at how you can operate successfully using short-term loans in your business.

Money Techniques that Build Wealth

For best results with short-term loans, use these wealth-building money techniques:

(a) Try to pay off a little—even 10 percent—every time you renew your loan.

(b) *Always* pay the interest due. If you don't, the bank or lender will call your loan; i.e., insist that you pay the entire amount you owe, *plus* all the interest due.

(c) Keep at least one bank account at the bank which grants you a short-term loan. This makes good business sense and can be beneficial for you.

(d) Keep in touch with the lender. Don't ignore his calls or letters. Why lose the friends who can help you the most?

(e) Try to "clean up"—pay off—your loan once a year, if you've been renewing it. Your lender will love you for it and each year he'll be willing to lend you more.

Banks and other lenders can be the friendliest people you'll ever meet—provided you realize they're human, just like yourself. Howard A. realized this when he borrowed $20,000 on a short-term loan to start an insurance company specializing in underwriting fire risks. His company boomed and he soon had the largest fire insurance company in the state. Within a few years Howard A. was buying out other companies. He also branched out to home and mortgage financing. Today Howard A. is worth some 300 million dollars. And he got his start with a short-term loan that grew to be worth 15,000 times its face amount!

"Being nice to bankers and other lenders really paid off for me," says Howard A. "I recommend this same approach to every beginning wealth builder. Don't get tough until you earn your first one hundred million dollars. Then you can afford to have your own way!"

Business Loan Secrets

In each chapter of this book I try to give you one or more financing secrets I've learned in my highly profitable business career. The secret you're about to learn is hardly known outside the brightly polished offices of the bank and finance company presidents. It is this:

A business loan can be made for any of hundreds of purposes. For this reason, you will find it easier to obtain a business loan than any other type of loan—if you have an established business.

Typical reasons for business loans are: finance new equipment, purchase inventory, repair business equipment or buildings, pay for current operations, pay off back bills, etc. A safe generalization is that you can borrow money for any legitimate business purpose. Banks and other lenders are delighted to lend money to a business because the chances of being repaid are much greater than with personal loans.

Putting the Secret to Work

Recently a beginning wealth builder (BWB), Clint T., borrowed $2,000 to pay for having his factory interior repainted. When Clint arrived in his office after receiving the loan, his telephone was ringing. He picked it up. His commodity futures broker was calling.

"Clint," he said, "if you sell pork bellies short today, I think that you can hit it big by early summer. Do you want to pick up one or two contracts?"

Clint looked around his office. The walls were dirty and needed painting badly. Yet his commodity broker had been right before. And the $2,000 check Clint had just received from the bank would cover three contracts—if he added a few dollars—because the price of a pork belly contract was $700. Clint decided that the painting could wait a few months. "Sell three pork belly contracts short," he told the broker. That was April 24th.

On June 11th the broker called again. "Clint," he said, "I think you'd be wise to cover those three pork belly contracts you shorted last April." (Covering is the buying of a commodity contract to replace a shorted contract; i.e., a borrowed contract which you sold as though you owned the contract.)

"How would I do if I covered now?" Clint asked.

"Oh, you'd make a profit of about four grand per contract," the broker replied.

"Cover me right now," Clint ordered.

Clint's actual profit per contract was $4,100, after commissions and other fees. Thus, he made a total of $12,300 in less than 50 days. When he repaid the bank the $2,000 he borrowed, Clint had more than $10,000 in cash, or a profit of over $200 per day for doing nothing while he had other people's money invested!

Clint had his entire office and factory repainted with the profits from his commodity sale. He attributes his success to the fact that business loans are made for a variety of purposes—for this reason the businessman usually has greater flexibility in the use of the funds he borrows.

Try Commercial Paper as a Money Source

If your business is organized as a corporation you should consider using *commercial paper* as a source of short-term money. Commercial paper is the name used for short-term (30-, 60-, 90-, 180-, 270-day) promissory notes sold by corporations to individuals or other corporations. These notes are unsecured; i.e., the corporation does not put up any collateral to guarantee payment of the note when it becomes due.

The usual interest rate on commercial paper is about 6 percent. Sometimes the rate will rise to 6.25, or slightly higher, when money is in great demand. When the demand for money falls the interest rate you have to pay usually declines to less than 6 percent.

What are the advantages of commercial paper to you? There are several:

- You can issue as much paper as you wish
- Repayment is made only when the note falls due
- Notes need no security behind them
- You can stop selling notes whenever you wish

Let's take a careful look at these advantages so we understand them better. Then we'll take a look at the disadvantages.

Borrow as Much as You Need

When you borrow for business purposes a bank or other lender will often say:

"Mr. BWB, you're a great guy and you have a marvelous future. But with conditions as they are today we can't lend you any more than _____ dollars."

And if you're like most BWBs, the amount the bank is willing to lend you is usually about $5,000 *less* than you really need. So you have to scramble around for the extra five grand which you may—or may not—find.

With commercial paper no such problem exists. You simply issue as much paper as you need. And, if you're suddenly short of funds, you just issue some more paper.

Rid Yourself of Monthly Repayment Blues

Commercial paper is *retired*—you pay off your note—at the *end* of the loan period. Thus, on a 270-day or nine-month note, you don't pay anything until the 270th day after you receive the money. This freedom from monthly repayments can give you greater room to maneuver and close deals.

Once your note falls due you must pay it off. But if you're short of funds because a deal you're working on is still underway, you can issue a new note to pay off your first note. Using this technique, you can go on issuing notes for years to cover your first note. But you have to pay the interest each time you pay off a note.

Make Your Business Your Security

You will often be asked to obtain a cosigner when you try to borrow large sums on a personal loan. The reason for this is that the lender wants more security. But with commercial paper:

Your business corporation is the only security you need; cosigners are unnecessary.

As you can see, commercial paper gives you greater freedom of action. You can operate as independently as you wish, without the interference of people who want to tell you how to run your business. Many of these people really know very little about your business or any other business.

Avoid Free Advice

You are either an ambitious BWB or an experienced business person. How do I know this? Because you're reading this book. That puts you in either category.

As such a person, please accept some business loan advice from someone who has been involved in numerous deals. This advice is:

Get as much help from accountants, lawyers, and other professionals as you can. Then make your own business decisions.

I can't stress this point too strongly. *Make your own decisions!*

As owner of your business you know what you want to do. The best lawyers and accountants can give you good advice, but *you must make the decisions!*

Keep one important fact in mind at all times:

While your business is small you know its details better than anyone else. Further, other people don't care as much about your business as you do.

So, get all the advice you need. But then do as you think best. After all, you have what the European businessman calls "the owner's eye"; that is, the drive to make *your* business grow big and strong. Few hired people have the same desire for *your* business.

This advice is particularly valid when you're thinking of issuing commercial paper to obtain business loans for your corporation. Plenty of people who know very little about loans, business procedures, or corporations will say, "No! Don't borrow that way. Borrow another way."

But when you ask "What other way?" they can't answer you. All these people know is that they're against the way you plan to borrow money. Always remember: *Make your own financial decisions.*

Know the Power of Business Loans

Two brothers borrowed $550 to open an ice-cream shop during a time when business conditions were poor. But their shop was so attractive they soon had to open another. Today they have some 170 shops doing a gross annual business of nearly 22 million dollars. That's not bad, particularly on an investment of 550 dollars! This is an excellent example of the power of business loans.

Wide experience leads me to believe that a business loan often brings the BWB more financial gain than any other type of loan. Why is this? Because:

A business loan—since it is made for profit-making purposes—is often put to better use than other loans. Hence, the business loan usually generates higher profits.

When a BWB takes out a personal loan he is less pressed to use it for business purposes. As a result, he may:

    (a) Delay investing the money
    (b) Spend some on himself
    (c) Invest in a different business
    (d) Lend some of the money to friends
    (e) Give some money to his family

If you want to use the magic power of business loans you must:

(a) Study potential investments you might make
(b) Choose the best investment for yourself
(c) Plan the steps that will make your investment grow
(d) Borrow the money you need
(e) Invest the borrowed money
(f) Follow your plan for making your money grow

Thus you can see that making borrowed money grow takes planning and hard work. But it isn't as difficult as it sounds. Why? Because:

Planning money and business growth is easy, once you form the habit. After that, you will plan every new venture.

Know Other Types of Business Loans

If you own a going business there are many other types of business loans for which you may be eligible. The loans include:

(a) Inventory loans
(b) Working capital loans
(c) Accounts receivable loans
(d) Disaster loans
(e) Mortgage loans
(f) Property improvement loans
(g) Equipment loans

Check with your bank or other lenders, such as insurance and finance companies, about the availability of these types of loans. You may be pleasantly surprised to learn that there is more money available for your business than you ever thought possible. When checking out different types of business loans keep one fact in mind at all times. This fact is:

Willingness to lend money depends on the amount of funds available. A lender who is short of funds today may have millions available tomorrow. So keep trying—don't give up!

To receive a monthly list of lenders who have funds available for business loans, subscribe to the newsletter *International Wealth Success*.

This monthly newsletter regularly lists numerous lenders—banks, insurance companies, finance companies, and factors—interested in placing money in the hands of business borrowers. You will also find many other features of this newsletter covering finder's fees, investment opportunities, overseas firms wanting to represent U.S. firms, international opportunities, mail-order businesses and offerings, foreign firms seeking U.S. exports, etc., profitable and interesting. Regular (one-year or longer) subscribers can run ads free of charge in the newsletter. These ads may help you locate the business capital you need.

Work with a Factor

A factor is an organization or person willing and able to lend money to a going business which has some form of current security to offer. Typical security acceptable to factors includes:

> Accounts receivable
> Work in process
> Inventory

Here's how a factor usually works with you.

Let's say you're in the toy-making business. You make toys for boys and girls and sell these toys to large department stores, discount houses, hobby stores, and to overseas outlets. We'll assume that the month is November and that you have accounts receivable of $34,000; that is, your various customers owe you $34,000 for toys you have shipped to them. Here's what your factor will do for you:

(1) Examine your shipping receipts
(2) Take copies of your bills
(3) Lend you $34,000, less a small service charge
(4) Collect the $34,000 owed you

Thus, a factor can help you because he is able to supply immediate cash for your accounts receivable, or for any other debts owed you in your business. You pay a small service fee for the convenience of receiving your cash quickly.

What happens if the factor isn't paid by your customer? This seldom happens—factors are expert bill collectors.

But if the factor can't collect, he may ask you to return the money which he lent you for the business bills which are now uncollectible. Or he may take his loss and charge you a much higher fee the next time you ask his assistance.

Note this important feature of factoring:

While a factor lends you money against business debts owed you, he cancels his loan to you as soon as he receives payment from your customer.

The self-cancelling feature of factoring is a distinct advantage to you. Why? Because it relieves you of the chore of keeping track of a number of debts.

Is Factoring a Good Business Practice?

There was a time when factoring was confined to marginal firms—those with very small or no cash reserves. This is no longer true. Today the biggest firms in the world are conscious of the advantages of factoring. So you'll find millions of firms—large and small—using factors.

Many modern firms are factoring to "turn the cash faster"—use their money more often each year. This technique builds high profits quickly. Thus:

One large factor reports that his clients increased their sales volume an average of nearly 48 percent in one year. Some of the clients increased their sales 500 percent using factoring and related services!

So if you have a company that's actively doing business, and you can use extra cash, try factoring. It could quickly put you on easy street.

How to Buy a Business Without Investing a Cent

"Your ideas are great," you say. "But there's just one catch—*I don't have a going business!* Further, I don't have the money to invest in, or buy, a business. So what am *I* to do?"

I have an answer for you. This answer is so good that it will:

(1) Give you a regular income
(2) Provide you with a going business

What more can you ask for, particularly when you don't have to invest anything—not a cent—except some of your time? Now here's the answer:

To obtain a going business for income and loan purposes, take over a business using promissory notes instead of cash.

"How does this work?" you ask. Here are the six steps you can follow to take over a business without a penny of investment.

(1) Decide what business you want to go into.

(2) Watch the ads in large newspapers, *International Wealth Success*, and magazines to find a business of the type that interests you.

(3) Contact the seller to learn how long the business has been for sale.

(4) Study the profit and loss and income statements of the business, if it has been for sale for more than one month.

(5) If these statements show that the business is earning a suitable profit, offer to take over the business at the *seller's price*, with no cash down. Instead of cash, offer a series of monthly promissory notes.

(6) Continue offering on suitable businesses until your offer is accepted by one seller.

What's the principle behind this technique? It's this:

When people have a business up for sale for a long time without selling it, they eventually may be willing to sell for no cash down, if they feel you will make a success of the business.

This technique is ideal for any BWB who is determined to build his fortune. Using this method, you can build your income from zero to fifty thousand dollars per year in just a few weeks. And if you're really ambitious, you can earn twice that during the first year you're using this method. For best results:

• Know the business you want to enter
• Work hard to impress the seller
• Keep looking—your big break may be just a day away
• Aim high—don't settle for second-best when you can get the best!

There's Money in Business Loans

Later chapters show you how and where to borrow money for other types of business loans. Continue reading to learn more about these valuable loan sources. You'll soon agree—there's money in business loans!

5

Make Compensating Balance Loans Work for You

One form of business loan—the compensating balance loan—is well worth looking into. Why? Because a compensating balance loan can:

- Help you borrow larger sums of money
- Get you your money faster
- Save you an embarrassing credit check
- Rid you of the need for cosigners

Let's see how the compensating balance loan works and how you can profit from it.

Know the Details of Compensating Balance Loans

With a compensating balance loan you

Borrow money from a lender and deposit this money in a bank in a business checking account. This deposit works as your compensating balance.

Let's say you borrow $10,000 for a compensating balance and deposit it in your business checking account.

"I'll be maintaining a balance of $10,000 or more in my business checking account," you quietly tell your banker.

"I'm delighted to hear that," he says with a smile. "If I can be of help, drop by to see me."

"Now that you mention it," you reply, "I'd like to know how much I can borrow using my $10,000 as a compensating balance."

"This bank uses the 20 percent rule; that is, your compensating balance must be at least 20 percent of your loan. So with a ten thousand dollar compensating balance you could borrow $10,000/0.2 = $50,000."

"Most interesting," you say slowly, thinking of how you could use that much money in your business.

As a guide, you can say for most banks that:

To find the amount you can borrow using a compensating balance, divide the balance amount you have available by the bank's percent requirement.

Here are the divisors to use for various percentage needs of different percent.

Bank's percent requirement	Use a divisor of:
10	0.10
20	0.20
30	0.30
40	0.40
50	0.50

Check Your Loan Know-How

As a quick review of your understanding of this method, here are three typical compensating balance situations you might wish to check out. The answers are given below.

YOUR COMPENSATING BALANCE SITUATIONS

(a) Your compensating balance = $30,000; bank's percent requirement = 30%; amount you can borrow = $_____ .

(b) You need $50,000 for your business. How much of a compensating balance must you deposit if the bank has a 20 percent requirement? $_____ .

(c) A banker tells you that he wants a $20,000 compensating balance deposit to back a $100,000 loan. This shows you that his percent requirement is ____ %.

ANSWERS

(a) You can borrow $30,000/0.30 = $100,000.
(b) A deposit of 0.20 ($50,000) = $10,000 is needed.
(c) The percent requirement is $20,000/$100,000 = 0.20, or 20 percent.

The three situations given above cover every arrangement you'll normally meet in compensating balance loans. Knowing this, you can easily figure how much to borrow.

Why Use a Compensating Balance?

There are a number of good business reasons for using a compensating balance. These reasons include:

(1) You can quickly establish better relations with your bank.

(2) You can borrow compensating balance funds quickly—sometimes faster than other funds.

(3) Your chances of having a compensating balance loan application approved are greater than for other types of loans.

(4) Banks like to lend on a compensating balance basis.

Let's take a quick look at each of these reasons to learn how and why they will help you.

Establish Better Banking Relations

"There's nothing as comforting as being on good terms with your banker," John M., president of one of the world's largest banks, told me in Chicago recently during a business lunch. "When your banker believes in you, there's no limit to what he'll do to try to help you. That's why it's important that every businessman be on the best terms with his bank."

Now, let's face reality. If you can obtain a five-figure ($10,000 or more) compensating balance loan (and I'm certain you can if you own your own business) any bank in the world will be delighted to have you deposit your compensating balance funds with them. The simple fact is this:

All banks are eternally looking for additional deposits. Your compensating balance funds are therefore most welcome.

When you tell a banker, "I'll be keeping a balance of ten thousand dollars in my business checking account," he immediately says to himself: "This is an important customer. I'd better treat him well enough not to lose him to another bank."

Treating you well enough includes:

(a) Lending you money when you need business funds
(b) Calling you when your account is short of money
(c) Explaining bank rules and regulations
(d) Tipping you off to important changes in bank rules
(e) Extending credit when you need it

There are many other ways in which a bank can treat you well. The best way to find out what these ways are is to establish good banking relations and learn. You won't be sorry—of that I'm certain because you'll have access to more money than you need! And that, to any Beginning Wealth Builder (BWB), is a heavenly situation.

Compensating Balance Loans Are Made Quickly

When you borrow money for compensating balance purposes the lender deposits the funds in your business checking account. The lender will probably ask you to sign a pledge stating that you will not withdraw (spend) the compensating balance.

Since the lender knows his money will be deposited directly in your bank, and since you sign the no-spending pledge *before* you receive the money, compensating balance loans are made quickly—usually within 24 to 48 hours after you apply.

But to be eligible for a compensating balance loan you must have your own going business. If you don't own a business now, but you would like to borrow compensating balance funds, then establish a going business using the techniques I gave you in earlier chapters of this book.

To learn which lenders offer compensating balance loans I suggest that you subscribe to *International Wealth Success*, which often lists lenders interested in making compensating balance loans.

Turn the Odds in Your Favor

For years I've made big money doing things that I know are acceptable to the public. Many times people say to me "Ty, why don't you write novels instead of self-help books? I'm sure you'd make a lot more money from novels!"

I patiently try to explain to these people that:

The greatest successes in life come when a person does those things in which the odds favor him.

The odds favor me when I write self-help books. Therefore, I write self-help books instead of novels. Further, I believe I am being of greater use to people when I write self-help books and this gives me immense satisfaction. So do those things for which the odds favor *you!*

With compensating balance loans the odds favor you. I've advised and worked with hundreds of BWBs interested in borrowing money. Also, I've borrowed large sums of money for many of my own business activities. And in every case—without fail—it was, and is, easier to obtain a compensating balance loan than any other type of loan.

So, if you own your own business, try a compensating balance loan. Then you may decide to quote Mike Todd to your friends because, like Mike, you can truly say "I've never been poor, only broke. Being poor is a frame of mind. Being broke is only a temporary situation."

Banks Like Compensating Balance Loans

Throughout this book I've tried to get one important point across. This point is:

Bankers are human—just like you and me. They want—and need—your business and mine. So never be afraid of a banker—he needs you.

A compensating balance customer is a valuable find for any banker. Why? Because you:

- Deposit money in the bank
- Maintain an account in the bank
- Do business with the bank
- May be a source of income for the bank

This is why banks prefer compensating balance loans over personal, mortgage, emergency, and many other types of loans. "Every bank," as one bank vice-president recently told me, "loves to get a 'piece of the action.' And that's exactly what happens when one of our compensating balance customers makes a bundle. He gives us more business, which means greater profits for us from that account. So send me every compensating balance customer you can find!"

What Compensating Balances Cost

As you've read this chapter you might have thought, "All this sounds great, but a compensating balance loan probably costs so much that I couldn't swing it."

It's true that a compensating balance loan *does* cost money. But so does any other loan. And the usual compensating balance loan, while it does cost a little more than the usual business loan, doesn't cost so much that it will put you out of business. If you figure a cost of 12 percent—$12 per $100 per year—for your compensating balance loan, you won't be far off. That's certainly a reasonable cost, in view of the many advantages a compensating balance loan offers you.

Expand to Revolving Credit

With a compensating balance, the bank turns over to you the money you borrow. You then use the money for whatever business purposes you wish.

Revolving credit is an arrangement whereby a bank or other lender sets aside a certain amount of money—say $20,000—as a credit to your business against which you can write checks. A $20,000 revolving credit account gives you the same amount of money as a $20,000 loan. But with revolving credit, the money stays in the possession of the bank until you are ready to use it.

Why do I mention revolving credit in this chapter on compensating balance loans? The answer to that is easy.

With a sum of money suitable for use as a compensating balance, you can often obtain revolving credit from several lenders at the the same time.

Thus, instead of $20,000 in revolving credit, as we mentioned above, you might be able to obtain three or five times as much from several lenders!

Pyramid Your Revolving Credit

Don't be satisfied with just one revolving credit account, if you have your own business. Instead, look for two or more lenders who will extend revolving credit to you. Here's how you can find several lenders:

(1) Check your bank. With a good record at your own bank you stand an excellent chance of obtaining revolving credit.

(2) Inquire at other local banks. Even if your application is turned down you'll learn what these banks require.

(3) Obtain a compensating balance loan, as discussed earlier in this chapter.

(4) Go back to the bank that seemed most friendly to you. Tell the credit officer that you'll deposit your compensating balance loan in his bank if he extends revolving credit to you. He will!

How Much Does Revolving Credit Cost?

Just like a compensating balance loan, revolving credit costs money. Why? Because the banker sets aside money for you. He can't be expected to do this unless he earns a profit. Further, since the usual revolving credit agreement runs for two years or longer (sometimes as long as 7 years) the lender has his money tied up for extended periods. Hence, he has to earn enough to justify using the money for this purpose instead of some other.

You pay three nominal charges for the usual revolving credit service. These charges are:

(1) Interest on the money you are using
(2) A commitment commission of 1/4 to 1/2 percent
(3) A small charge for the money held in reserve

Taken together, these small charges won't make your cost of money excessive. Most revolving credit agreements will cost you less than 1 percent per month. This cost includes *all* the three charges listed above.

Use Other Collateral

The compensating balance isn't the only collateral you can use for revolving credit. Other collateral often used, and which you can use, includes:

(a) Bills of lading; i.e., finished goods in transit which have a marketable value
(b) Warehouse receipts for goods you have in storage
(c) Accounts and notes receivable; i.e., money people owe you
(d) Trust receipts used for floor plan and similar financing

Using any collateral of this or a similar type you can obtain revolving credit for periods ranging between two and seven years. Since revolving credit agreements are seldom cancelled, you can easily build your fortune using the magic of OPM obtained this way. (The only reason a lender cancels a revolving credit agreement is because a borrower doesn't live up to the terms of the agreement.)

Seven Who Hit It Big

Here are the experiences of seven people, most of them much like you, who hit the big money using other people's money. Learn from their wealth stories how you, a BWB, can go from little or no money to great wealth in a short time, using OPM. Resolve, here and now, to extract yourself from a low-income, poor cash-flow situation. Replace poverty with riches. Here's how seven people did exactly that.

FINANCING PEOPLE PAYS OFF

Murray T. worked as an electrician on large construction jobs. While he enjoyed his work and the high hourly pay that he earned, Murray wanted more from life. Specifically, Murray wanted a business of his own. Yet he didn't want to get himself tied up with a factory, a payroll, employment taxes, etc.

To prepare himself for his own business, Murray read a large number of books on money and finance. It was during this reading that Murray discovered the compensating balance loan. "This type of loan will give me the money I need," Murray said. "Now I have to find a way to put this money to work to earn money for me!"

Several days later Murray was at work on a large office building construction project. During the lunch break on the thirty-second floor of the skyscraper, Murray was munching his sandwich and staring out over the city. Suddenly a thought hit him. Why couldn't he use the money he borrowed to finance other beginning wealth builders? Almost every man Murray worked with wanted to set up his own business. Murray would become their banker, lending them money to set up their businesses. And part of his fee would be a "piece" of each business. This could be in the form of shares of stock or a profit sharing plan. Here's what Murray did. He:

1. Set up his own small-business consulting firm.
2. Applied for two $5,000 personal loans.
3. Told his friends he was ready to finance them.
4. Borrowed $50,000 using his $10,000 as a compensating balance.
5. Lent money to beginning and experienced businessmen.

Within a year Murray had a steady income from the small businesses he financed and from interest on loans he made to beginning wealth builders. In less than two years he repaid the $10,000 he used as the basis for his compensating balance loan. Today Murray has an income of more than $50,000 per year from his finance business. Now people owe him, instead of his owing others. Further, he has "a piece"—he owns a part of some 18 businesses. Yet he doesn't work even a minute a month at any of these businesses!

BECOME A SHOPPING-CENTER MAGNATE

Cecil T. heard of a busy shopping center for sale in his area. Checking into the financial details of the center, he found it highly attractive, except for one detail—the $100,000 down payment required. Cecil didn't have even $1,000, yet he was determined to buy the shopping center. Here's what Cecil T. did. He:

1. Set up a real-estate operating company.
2. Applied for $20,000 in personal loans.
3. Used his real-estate company as collateral for the above loans.
4. Borrowed $100,000 using the $20,000 as compensating balance funds.
5. Bought the shopping center.
6. Used the shopping-center cash flow to pay off the loans.
7. Applied the same principle to the purchase of three other centers as collateral for new loans.

Today Cecil T. owns four highly profitable shopping centers. His net income exceeds $100,000 per year. Yet he spends less than one month a year supervising his investments!

FAST PROFITS IN THE STOCK MARKET

The closer you get to business the more you understand the meaning of the expression *business risk*. You can spend months, or years, pretending to be in business. But the moment you put your money on the line, the faster you realize what it means to take a business risk.

Herb F. is a mailman, who works in a little town in the Midwest. All his life Herb has been interested in the stock market. But his small mailman's income has prevented him from making a big killing in the market.

Recently, Herb heard of a new, small computer software company that was going public for the first time. Herb studied the company and concluded that it was soundly managed. Further, Herb felt he could make a big profit if he:

    (a) Could borrow some money.
    (b) Buy the computer company stock.
    (c) Sell the stock after it rose in value.

But Herb wasn't in business. The largest loan he could get was a $1,000 personal loan. Herb pondered his problem.

One day, on his postal route, Herb met the president of a small local store. Herb mentioned the computer company to the president. "Can you get me in on that?" the president asked excitedly. "I'd be delighted to put up a couple of thousand dollars, if you could get me in on the deal."

That's when the idea hit Herb. *Form an investment syndicate and take a share of the profits,* was the thought that flashed through Herb's mind. Here's what Herb did.

(1) Talked ten men into putting up a total of $40,000 for stock purchases.

(2) Contacted the broker handling the stock and told him he wanted $40,000 worth.

(3) Drew up a profit-sharing agreement with the people in his syndicate specifying that he'd get 50 percent of any profits.

The stock came on the market at $10 per share. Within three days the stock jumped to $70 per share. Herb bought 4,000 shares at $10 per share, using the $40,000 of syndicate money. Within three days the value of these shares rose to $280,000. So Herb and his backers had a profit of $240,000 (= $280,000–40,000). Since Herb was to get half the profit, his share was $120,000, less the broker's commission, which was small.

But instead of taking his profit directly by selling the shares, Herb used his shares as collateral for a compensating balance loan. Herb invested the money he obtained from this loan, $600,000, in a highly profitable motel. Today he's on easy street. Yet it took him only a few weeks to hit it big!

GET IN ON EXPLOSIVE GROWTH

Herb's stock market exploits sound great. Yet you could have done better than Herb in the stock market if you followed Ernie F., another BWB, recently. If you were close to Ernie F., you would have watched a $7.25 investment grow to $260 in four months. That's a growth of 3,500 percent! Here's what Ernie did. He:

(1) Decided to make his big money in the stock market.

(2) Chose hot new issues as his specialty.

(3) Sought several brokers handling new issues.

(4) Told the brokers of his new-issue interest.

Ernie borrowed a total of $20,000 from several banks, floating a $5,000 personal loan at each bank. Since his credit rating was a bit shaky, Ernie obtained four cosigners for his notes. As an incentive to his cosigners, Ernie promised each a 1 percent share of the profits he earned on the borrowed money he invested.

Shortly after he obtained the loans, Ernie received a call from one of his brokers. "Would you be interested in 3,000 shares of a hot new issue at $7.25 each?" he asked Ernie.

"Positively," Ernie replied. "But I have enough cash for only about 2,800 shares."

"Don't worry," the broker said. "We'll use the shares you buy as collateral for the other two hundred shares."

Ernie bought the 3,000 shares in March. By June of the same year—just four months later—Ernie's $20,000 investment grew to $780,000. That's a profit of some $760,000 in four months! "If I could have bought just a few more shares, I could have become a millionaire in four months," Ernie told me recently.

What is the key to Ernie's and Herb's stock market profits? Is it new issues, new companies, or something else? The key is this:

You can obtain favored treatment from brokers, and have a better chance to make big money if you have a large sum to invest in a stock.

Why is this true? The reason is that brokers are salesmen. They earn their income by selling stock. So when you walk in with $10,000 or more to invest in stocks, the broker is anxious to make, and keep, you as his customer. That's why he'll give you a break on new stocks that can zoom through the roof. Others regularly make big money this way—so can you. The only difference is that you'll make it on OPM.

GAME INVENTOR HITS IT BIG

Most of us play games of some kind or other. For instance, some men like chess; others enjoy poker; still others play scrabble or similar games. Pat L. enjoys inventing games as much as he enjoys playing them. So in the last few years, Pat invented several successful games. Here's how Pat hit the big money with his games. He:

(1) Borrowed enough money to print and box his first game
(2) Assembled the game in his home in his spare time
(3) Acting as his own salesman, sold, and still sells, his games to department stores

Why is Pat in the big money just a few years after he started working on his games? There are several reasons. Pat's income is big because:

(a) He took all the risks (inventing, printing, boxing, and selling) himself.

(b) Since he does his own selling, his unit profit is higher because he uses no distributors.

(c) Sales are easier to make because a larger discount can be offered the stores.

(d) Being in constant touch with his market, he can adjust prices as necessary to increase sales.

RAW LAND PAYS HUGE PROFITS

"Rental real estate is okay for some people," Clyde C. says. "But I prefer raw land because it doesn't spring any leaks in the plumbing pipes. What's more, the profit potential from raw land is greater than from any other type of real estate. Why? Because when people buy raw land they're purchasing for the future. And most people are willing to pay more for their future dreams than they are for what they can see today!"

How should you purchase raw land to earn big profits for yourself? Here are four profit-laden tips that regularly earn millions for BWBs throughout the world.

(1) Use OPM to finance your raw-land buys.

(2) Buy land in the path of population growth.

(3) Follow a steady buying and selling program.

(4) Use the profits from one sale to finance the next buy.

This book shows you hundreds of ways to borrow money you can use to purchase raw land. Clyde C. used a number of these ways to borrow money while building a fortune from raw-land deals.

Once you know how to borrow the money you need, the next most important step is determining the direction of population growth in the area where you're buying. Here are five steps useful in predicting the direction of population growth.

(1) Obtain a large-scale map of the entire area. Since most raw-land deals occur around cities, the city maps available free from gas stations are usually suitable.

(2) Drive around the city. Look for new housing developments, shopping centers, industrial plants, etc. Mark a dot on the map for

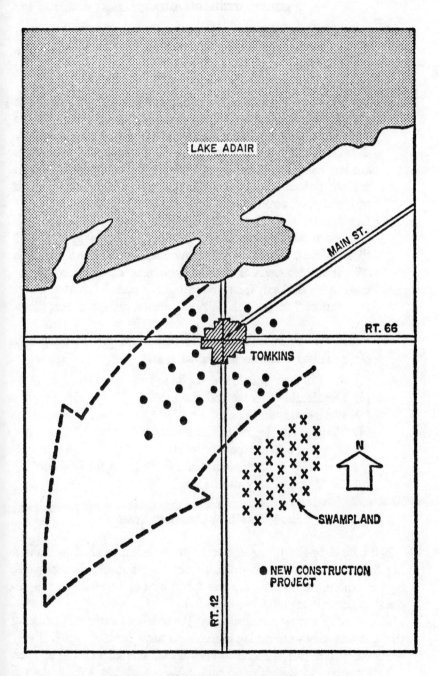

Figure 5-1: Plot of the expansion of a city

each new construction project you see. (If you can't drive, buy copies of your local papers and read the real estate pages. Use the same dot system for each new construction project that is advertised or written about.)

(3) Try to detect any trends you can in the direction of population growth. Figure 5-1 shows a map of the city of Tomkins with the new construction projects a BWB marked on it. This map clearly shows that this city is expanding to the southwest because there are far more new construction projects in this direction than in any other. Indicate the probable direction of population growth with a dashed arrow like that shown in Fig. 5-1.

(4) Check with real-estate brokers for their opinion of the probable future direction of population growth. You'll usually find that their opinions will agree with your map, unless there are some natural barriers—such as swamps, rock quarries, or other obstructions which markedly increase construction costs. Thus, the swamp southeast of Tomkins will delay population growth in that direction.

(5) Verify the probable direction of population growth using any other method available to you, such as:

(a) State highway construction plans

(b) Electric utility power line extensions

(c) Water-main extensions

(d) Housing development announcements

(e) Shopping-center expansion plans

(f) Any other announcements of specific plans for land use

(g) Town and county deed records

BIG-MONEY LOW-OVERHEAD PLAN

Betty B., a bright young computer programmer, wanted to make a big income quickly. But she didn't want to get involved in payrolls, high overhead, and other problems faced by big business. So she decided to concentrate on a low-overhead plan.

One evening, during a dinner party, she overhead two men discussing the problems they were having in picking a name for a company. "Every name we tried to use had already been taken," one man said to another.

This remark set Betty's mind racing. In a flash she said to herself "Why couldn't I register company names with the state and then sell the names when real, live companies want them?"

Betty investigated further. She learned that she could form a corporation in her state for $70. Since Betty wasn't forming the corporations to operate them, but only to have the name of the corporation under her control, an attorney was unnecessary. So here's what Betty did:

(1) Borrowed $5,000 on a personal loan from a local bank.
(2) Formed 71 corporations.
(3) Used the word *computer* in the name of each corporation.

Why did Betty use the word *computer* in the name of each of her corporations? Because many new computer companies were being formed at that time. So corporate names with the word computer in them were in great demand. Here's Betty's sales record:

Month No.	Sales, $
1	0
2	0
3	50
4	0
5	1,100
6	27,000
7	58,000
8	65,000
9	104,000
10	3,000
11	4,500
12	3,200

Note that within six months Betty had sold nearly $30,000 worth of corporate names. And in the second six months she sold $237,700 worth of names! Yet all this resulted from only $5,000 worth of OPM!

Give Yourself a $100,000-Per-Year Raise

Using a compensating balance loan you can easily borrow $100,000 a year—*each year*—for the next ten years, or more. And if you take a moment to multiply $100,000 by 10 you'll find that you get $1,000,000! That's real money, you say? It most certainly is!

How can you work this plan to give yourself a $100,000-per-year raise? Take these six steps:

(1) Register a company name in your state. (Cost: $2 to $10)
(2) Have company letterhead printed. (Cost: $10 to $15)
(3) Borrow $20,000 on one or more personal loans using the techniques described earlier.

(4) Deposit the $20,000 as a compensating balance for a $100,000 loan.

(5) During the first year, invest the $100,000 you borrowed and use the income from this investment to pay off part of the $20,000 and $100,000 loans, and build up another $20,000 nest egg.

(6) Follow the same procedure in the second, third, fourth, etc., years, i.e., use your $20,000 nest egg to borrow another $100,000 each year.

"This can't work," you say? "Why can't it?" I ask you. "Because. . . ." you pause.

Good thinking, I say to you. Your mind, as a result of reading this book and because you're so interested in earning a big fortune, is now seeking the reasons why a money plan will, or will not, work.

For this plan to work, one—and only one—condition must prevail. This is:

To make money on OPM, you must be able to invest the OPM so that it earns a higher rate of return than the rate of interest you pay.

Let's see how this works for our compensating balance plan.

Make OPM Work for You

To start, we'll say your true rate of interest on the $20,000 personal loan is 10 percent. (Actually, as you saw earlier in this book, the true rate of interest on a signature personal loan is a little more than 9 percent.) Using 10 percent, your annual interest cost on the $20,000 loan would be 0.10 ($20,000) = $2,000.

Your annual interest rate on the compensating balance loan would run between 6 and 8 percent at a large city bank. Using 7 percent, your annual interest charge on the $100,000 loan would be 0.07 ($100,000) = $7,000.

You now know that your annual interest costs for these loans is $2,000 + $7,000 = $9,000. This amount must be paid to the banks during the first year. In addition, you must pay back some of the principal on the loans. (During the second, and any later, year, the interest on the $100,000 loan will decrease if you've paid off some of the principal.)

The principal payment on your $20,000 loan will be $6,700, closely, per year. On the $100,000 loan, you'd have to repay at least $20,000 per year on the principal. So your total principal repayments will be $6,700 + $20,000 = $26,700; say $27,000. Adding the $9,000 annual interest payments which you must make gives: $27,000 + $9,000 = $36,000, the total annual debt repayment that must be made during the first year

Let's say you can invest your $100,000 so that:

(1) The net income to you after taxes will be $56,000.

(2) The time required to supervise your investment is 8 hours per week, or about 400 hours per year.

(3) You have other business interests so the income from the investment can be used as you wish.

With a net income of $56,000 per year from the $100,000 compensating balance loan investment, and debt repayments of $36,000 per year, you have a net cash flow of: $56,000–$36,000 = $20,000 per year. You can use this as you wish—for further investment, for larger debt repayments, or for fun. Take your choice—the money is yours.

Shorten the Years to Your Fortune

Let's say you want to borrow only $500,000 over a five-year period instead of the $1 million in 10 years described above. With the same investment each year, as above—$100,000 which returns $56,000 profit—this is how your plan will work out:

Year	Net cash flow, $	Invested for new compensating balance loan, $	Net income to you, $
1	20,000	20,000	0
2	40,000	20,000	20,000
3	60,000	20,000	40,000
4	80,000	20,000	60,000
5	100,000	20,000	80,000

Thus, you'd be earning $80,000 per year at the end of four years. But what's better yet is that your plan is self-liquidating; i.e., it pays its own way while earning you a profit. And, interestingly, your yearly income when your debts are repaid on your first two loans will be $116,000. Further, your income will increase by $36,000 per year each time you pay off a set of loans. Also, I ignored the reduction in interest charge on your compensating balance loans during the second, and later, years. This would increase your annual income somewhat, making the whole technique more attractive.

Put the Compensating Balance to Work

You *can* get rich using one or more compensating balance loans. This chapter will get you started. Put the techniques given here to work and you'll be wealthy sooner than you think!

6

Try the Anything Loan

Most of the people who come to me to ask my advice about business have one major problem—*they need capital*. And most of them, I'm sorry to say, think negatively about their chances of obtaining the capital they need.

Know Who Lends Money

"Who'd ever lend *me* that much money?" many of these Beginning Wealth Builders (BWBs) wail.

"Plenty of banks, finance companies, venture-capital firms, or private individuals," is my usual reply. "Why, I know of one finance company that alone makes 4,000 loans per day!"

When the BWB hears this his eyes get shiny. "Then you mean there's really a chance for me," he breathes, with a surge of hope.

"Millions of chances for millions of dollars," I laugh. Just remember what Julian S. Myrick, who built several fortunes, said: "There are more chances to get rich today than ever before in history. All you need is a little know-how and some borrowed money!"

Rent Yourself the Money You Need

Earlier I told you that I'm president of a million-dollar lending organization. I'm also a member of the board of directors of the same lending organization.

Do you know what we do at most of our monthly board-of-directors meetings? We sit around and worry—yes, worry—about why we aren't making more loans! Truly, I mean this; we are crying for people to borrow our money. We have money sitting in banks all over the United

States. And our biggest problem is to find suitable people to "rent" this money for a month, a year, two years, etc.

Is this problem unique to our lending organization? No! Thousands of other lenders:

(1) Are actively seeking people who will borrow money.
(2) Spend millions of dollars *advertising* for borrowers.
(3) Dream up reasons why you *should* borrow.
(4) Take greater lending risks than ever before.

Think of borrowing as "renting" of money. If you do, you'll find thousands of "landlords" ready to rent you almost any amount of money you need.

Get in on the Competitive Money Race

In our lending organization we spend hours every month trying to figure ways of beating the competition. Should we:

(a) Lower our interest rates?
(b) Give away gifts to borrowers?
(c) Make interest refunds?
(d) Extend our loan periods?
(e) Reduce the needed qualifications for loans?
(f) Make more than one loan to a borrower?

These, and similar questions, plague us. Why? Because there's so much competition to *make* loans. We compete with banks, finance companies, private lenders, etc. Each does a good job of promoting its services. But they are all competing for the loan *you* want someone to make. They're fighting one another, in a business way, to lend you money! What a dream world for the BWB.

How can you get in on the competitive money race? That's easy—and inexpensive. Here are the eight steps you should take.

(1) Decide how much money you need.
(2) Prepare a comprehensive financial résumé of yourself, emphasizing your good points.
(3) Study publications listing sources of capital. *International Wealth Success*, the *Wall Street Journal*, the *New York Times*, etc. are all good sources of this information.
(4) Contact the finance sources that interest you; ask for their descriptive brochures.
(5) Study the brochures you obtain. A careful reading of the brochures will show which organizations are most anxious to lend money.

(6) Make an appointment by phone or mail with the loan officer in the organization you select.

(7) Discuss your financial needs with the loan officer.

(8) Obtain the loan from the organization offering the best deal.

Try the <u>Anything</u> Loan

"Now," you say, "what does all this talk about competition and *your* lending problems have to do with *my* borrowing problem?"

Just this. In their hectic scramble for more and more business, lenders have sought more and more reasons for inducing *you* to borrow their money. And the best example of the great desire to lend money is the *anything* loan recently dreamed up by a number of banks.

What is the *anything* loan? Its just what its name says—a loan for *anything* you want, need, like, or desire. The only requirement on the reason for the loan is that the purpose of the loan be constructive. Thus, a bank won't lend money to be used to bet at the race tracks, Las Vegas or Monte Carlo casino tables, etc. But the bank will lend you money for almost *anything* else.

Why Is the <u>Anything</u> Loan Important?

To answer this question, I have to tell you a little about my business deals. I've earned a large amount of money from numerous businesses. and continue to do so. So, friend, I say most humbly, I must be doing something right! That something, besides hard work, is what I want to reveal to you. The fact that you want to work hard to earn a big fortune is revealed by your act of reading this book.

What is the something that is so important? It is this:

Where financing of a new or existing business venture is required and one loan isn't enough to furnish the money needed, use multiple loans.

The multiple-loan technique, which I "discovered," put me into the big money. Once I was in the big money and began to travel to the business capitals of the world—London, Stockholm, Copenhagen, Rome, Paris—I learned that my great financing "discovery" was really nothing new. Successful businessmen everywhere use multiple loans when they're short of cash.

Now, your *anything* loan is important because it gives you another valid *reason* and *source* for capital. And remember this:

Whenever you have a suitable reason for needing money, and know of a source that wants to lend money, your mission is half accomplished—the money is nearly in your hands.

Another important reason why the *anything* loan is vital to many BWBs is this:

When a person obtains his first loan quickly and easily, he builds a positive mental attitude towards borrowing for business purposes. This positive attitude makes it easier for him to obtain other loans in the future.

Limit Your Loans, if You Can

Recognize, here and now, that I'm *not* recommending that you always take out multiple loans.

If one loan will give you enough capital, then by all means, use only one loan. W. Clement Stone, the well-known insurance executive and author, started his wealth building with a capital of $100. Today his fortune exceeds $300 million. Such an enormous expansion of wealth clearly indicates the grow-power of money invested in the right business.

While some BWBs can get by nicely with just one loan, many need more money than is available from one loan. That's when I recommend that you use two or more loans, one of which is your *anything* loan.

Twelve Good Reasons for Borrowing

The usual *anything* loan is a personal note; i.e., you sign the note and you are personally responsible for repaying the money. Even if you take out an *anything* loan for business purposes, the bank will probably ask you to sign the note. Don't worry about such a request—almost every bank or other lender will require that you be personally responsible for loans when your business is still small. Once your business grows to a large enough size—about $1 million per year—you can borrow for the business without having to sign a note pledging your personal credit. When you reach that large a size you'll know everything you should about borrowing money and you won't need my advice.

But to go from little cash to $1 million is a giant step. Like the first step of a child, the BWB needs the largest amount of help with his first business step. This book aims at giving you all the help you need for this and every other step on your way to a great fortune.

One big area of help I can offer you here is supplying good, acceptable reasons for borrowing money for business use. Though I can't explain why the following is so, most BWBs have difficulty finding suitable reasons for borrowing money for business purposes. Then, should they meet a tough loan officer when they apply for their first loan, their application is turned down. This discourages the BWB, and he may give up his drive for wealth. To prevent this kind of discouragement and failure, here are 12 sure-fire reasons for borrowing for *business* purposes:

    (1) To buy an interest in another business
    (2) Build up inventory
    (3) Add new product lines
    (4) Expand existing product lines
    (5) Enlarge or expand production
    (6) Save money by increasing operating efficiency
    (7) Finance new equipment or buildings
    (8) Repair existing facilities
    (9) Modernize existing equipment or buildings
    (10) Buy out a partner
    (11) Finance accounts receivable
    (12) Pay for advertising or sales promotion

Try to use one, or a combination of two or more, of these reasons the next time you apply for a business loan. I'm sure you'll be delighted with the results.

Know the Six C's of Credit

Many lenders use the six C's of credit when they evaluate your application for an *anything* loan. If you know these six C's, you have a much better chance of having every loan application approved quickly and effortlessly. Here are the six C's, along with the facts you should know about each:

    (1) Character (yours)
    (2) Capital (you have in your business)
    (3) Capacity (your managerial ability)
    (4) Collateral (security you can offer)
    (5) Circumstances (surrounding the loan)
    (6) Coverage (life insurance on you)

Let's take a closer look at each C in this list.

A GOOD CHARACTER PAYS OFF

Character means two things to the lender: *(a)* that you are a man of your word; i.e., you will repay your loan in the manner agreed upon, and *(b)* that you will do everything possible to conserve the assets of your business so you can pay off the loan.

Knowing what a lender is looking for in terms of your character, you should:

(1) Emphasize your reliability and honesty.
(2) Show how carefully you manage money.
(3) Cite any quick loan payoffs you have made.
(4) Give examples of your financial and personal sincerity.

USE THE NO-CAPITAL WAY TO WEALTH

Capital you have invested in your business is extremely important to a prospective lender. Why? Because if you don't have enough faith in your business to invest your own money in the business, why should the lender invest his?

"But," you say, "I don't have *any* capital to invest in my business. So how can I show a lender that I'm convinced this business will make a fortune for someone?"

That's easy. When you don't have capital, substitute what you *do* have—time and labor. How can you invest time and labor? Here are a number of constructive and profitable ways using what I call the No-Capital Way to Wealth.

(1) Draw up financial plans for the business. Prepare a financial plan for each year for the next five years. Show your expected income and expenses for each year.
(2) Survey the market for your product, service, or other business offering. Prepare a written study showing which firms are in the business, what their annual income is, and how much of their business you could capture.
(3) Use your ingenuity. Where you don't know and can't obtain an important fact or figure—like annual sales of a competitor—make an approximation. With careful research and good judgment, you will often be able to make extremely accurate estimates of missing data.

(4) Have your financial plans neatly typed and bound, ready for presentation to a lender. Often, your neatness and precise thinking will make the difference between getting a loan and being refused.

Build Your Management Skills

Let's say you're a top-notch machinist. You're so good all your friends tell you that "you'd make a million if you opened your own business." At first you scoff at such talk. But after awhile you hear it from so many friends that you begin to believe them. Before you rush out to buy or start a business, stop and recognize this key fact:

The fact that a person is a capable mechanic or technician doesn't necessarily mean that this person is also a competent manager. The two activities require different skills.

Let's see what a competent business manager does. Typical work most managers perform includes:

> *Planning* their business activities
> *Organizing* their business resources
> *Motivating* their associates and employees
> *Controlling* their business costs

A manager gets his work done *through* other people. Bank loan officers know this because they are closer to management problems in all types of firms than most businessmen are. So when you apply for a loan, emphasize your managerial skills—how you plan, organize, motivate, and control the work of a profit-making activity. Remember—your capacity to manage is one of the important C's of credit.

Use Your Collateral

Lenders will accept many kinds of collateral as backing for your business loan. Typical collateral used for business loans includes:

- Machinery
- Buildings
- Inventory
- Stocks, bonds
- Cosigners

Collateral is important to a lender because:

A borrower who has collateral is thought to have proven himself in the business world. It is twice as easy to borrow when you have collateral, compared with not having it.

While cosigners are not officially classed as collateral by lenders, they serve the same purpose; i.e., they give the lender greater confidence that his loan will be repaid in the event something happens to you.

Earlier in this book you learned how to make the most effective use of cosigners. Review those hints now so you can borrow the largest amount of money for which you are eligible, based on your cosigners.

MAKE THE MOST OF CIRCUMSTANCES

A lender will look at your circumstances when you apply for a loan. Thus, two young men with a total of $800 between them recently applied for a loan of $500,000 to start a computer-controlled employment agency. The bank loan officer laughed at them. Why?

Because the circumstances of the loan; i.e.

- Two young, inexperienced men
- An untried, unproven business idea
- No collateral
- Little starting capital

made the amount of money requested completely unrealistic.

Yet all was not lost. By joining with a small firm that was going public—selling its stock to the public—these two young men were able to obtain $5 million instead of the $500,000 they were trying to borrow! So you see, just the process of seeking business funds can lead to interesting and profitable results. Incidentally, the time between the first loan application and the $5 million stock issue was four months. How would you like to go from $800 to $5 million in four months? It *can* and *is* being done by people who use their heads when borrowing money.

Remember—when seeking business funds, make the most of the circumstances in which you find yourself!

HAVE ENOUGH INSURANCE

Lenders recognize that life is an unpredictable situation. A person who looks healthy today may be dead tomorrow. To protect themselves, lenders insist that borrowers be covered by life insurance.

The cheapest form of life insurance you can buy is *term insurance.* This type of insurance gives you the protection you need without high premium payments. So if you plan to borrow a large sum of money, consider taking out a suitable term policy but don't pay on the policy until you're sure the loan will be granted.

Some lenders, particularly banks, will issue an insurance policy with your loan. There is a nominal charge for this coverage and it is money well spent. If the lender insists on such an insurance policy, *don't* argue. Accept it and be thankful. The amount the insurance policy adds to your monthly loan payment is insignificant.

Develop a Positive Outlook

The *anything* loan can put you on the glorious road to great wealth on other people's money—if you adopt a positive outlook.

You must believe you can borrow the money you need—and you will. Be positive and the world swings with you.

How can you develop the right outlook to ensure your success in the search for business funds? Here are a few useful hints that regularly work for others who, like yourself, seek to borrow money to make money. During my consulting sessions with beginning wealth builders I tell them:

(1) Millions of loans are made every business day. Your loan can easily be one of these.

(2) Act confident when you apply for your loan. Don't beg—just ask for what you want.

(3) Keep telling yourself: "The bank is more anxious to make this loan than I am." And the truth is that the bank is!

(4) Be friendly with the loan officer. If he wants to talk, let him! Allow him to be as big a big-shot as he wants, in his own eyes, as long as you get *your* money.

(5) Keep trying—don't give up. If one lender turns you down, try another. The prize goes to the strong, so never give up. You'll get your money, sooner or later, if you keep trying.

Learn from Every Interview

Never dismiss a loan interview without sitting down to analyze what went right and what went wrong.

Cecil K. was, in my opinion, in the poorest financial condition of any BWB I've ever met. He owed money to everyone, had a sickly wife, and two children who should have been doing better in school. Yet Cecil was able to borrow $20,000 from several banks using four *anything* loans.

Under my guidance, Cecil paid off most of his debts, put his wife in the care of a medical specialist, and enrolled his children in a private school. With these tasks finished, Cecil turned to his business ideas.

Cecil's dream was to own a mail-order business. "Which would you rather do—start with a preprinted mail-order catalog or find your own products?" I asked Cecil.

"I'd rather find my own products," he replied.

"Good, I'm glad to hear that," I said. "You'll work harder finding your own products, but you have an exclusive market which can lead to greater sales and higher profits. And, after all, Cecil, *profit* is the name of the mail-order game."

"It sure is," he laughed, "particularly if you have my debts and problems."

"Let's not worry about your personal problems," I said. "Instead, let's get you set up in a profitable business. Once we do that, I'm sure your personal problems will disappear."

"So, let's get going," Cecil said, with great enthusiasm.

How to Find Saleable Products

"What do you like to do most in your spare time?" I asked Cecil.

"Fish," he replied instantly.

"Good; what items would help you catch more fish?"

"Better lures," he immediately replied.

"Anything else?"

"Oh, possibly a specially made rod, better hooks, and, of course, better lures."

"You keep coming back to lures, Cecil. They seem to be your main interest."

"That's right," he said. "Every fisherman dreams of owning an ideal lure."

"Let's see if we can develop one," I suggested.

Check a Product's Potential

Since any product you or any other BWB develops is the result of *your* thoughts, you are better prepared to check its sales potential than anyone else in the world. Here's a useful market checklist to guide your thinking when considering the potential market for any product. It's the same one I gave to Cecil to help him check out his lures.

PRODUCT MARKET CHECKLIST

	YES	NO
1. Are competitive products available?	—	—
2. Does this product have one key feature?	—	—
3. Is this product better than the competition?	—	—
4. Would you buy this product to use?	—	—
5. Is this product priced higher than the competition?	—	—
6. Will this product outlast its competition?	—	—
7. Can the product be advertised?	—	—
8. Is the product difficult to manufacture?	—	—
9. Will you be the exclusive distributor of the product?	—	—
10. Can you get free promotion for the product?	—	—

You should have at least six *yes* checks to ensure success for your product. If items 1, 5, and 8 have *no* checks, and you have six or more *yes* checks, then you have a product that could be a real winner. And, friend, *there's nothing as exhilarating as having your own fast-selling mail-order product which you finance with OPM.* And the *anything* loan can be *your* source of OPM. In addition to a saleable product and OPM, you need, like Cecil did, at least one good friend.

Count on Your Good Friend

Every one of my hundreds of thousands of readers is a good friend of mine. Why? Because the people who read my books think like I do; that is, they are entranced with the idea of earning a big fortune. Since you are reading this book, *you are a good friend of mine!*

Test the Market for Your Product

In dealing with all sorts of products (including services) in hundreds of different markets I've learned that the key to success is this:

Test market your product or service before you invest a cent in manufacturing facilities or inventory.

Why spend large sums of money for machinery or inventory before you have to? Conserve your capital! Make every dollar you invest in a business do the maximum work possible. By market testing your product you get that extra zing that means the difference between success and failure. Here's how you can market test any product, and how I had Cecil market test his lures.

(1) Prepare a new product release for the magazines serving the field in which the product will be sold (in Cecil's case, the fishing, sporting, and outdoor magazines).

(2) Be *certain* to include, as part of the release, at least one glossy photograph of the product you are selling, and the price of the product. If you are selling a service instead of a product, use a photo of the service man performing a typical task. State the price for a typical service period—say one month.

(3) Send your new-product or new-service release to every magazine directly in the field of your major interest (fishing in Cecil's case) and to every other magazine that might be interested. (For most products and services, you should be able to send your release to at least 100 magazines.) If each magazine has an average readership (circulation) of 50,000 persons, your product or service will be promoted to 100 magazines $\times$ 50,000 persons per magazine = 5,000,000 people. The only cost to *you* will be about $3.00 for printing the 100 new-product releases, plus about $22 for postage, photos, and envelopes. Thus, the total cost to you of the release, and the publicity it generates, should not exceed about 25 dollars. Certainly, you can afford this amount of investment in your future fortune!

(4) Keep a record of the orders and inquiries you receive about your new product or service. If you receive a one-tenth of one percent response; that is, 5,000 total orders and inquiries when the readership of the magazines is 5,000,000 persons—you have a real mailorder moneymaker on your hands. With this size, or a larger, response, you can feel safe in going ahead with a full-scale manufacturing and marketing program. This is exactly what Cecil did, except that his response (some 3,000 orders and 12,000 inquiries) was so large that he hired a manufacturer to make his product while he concentrated on marketing the lures through the mail and in stores. Incidentally, Cecil received $21,000 in orders for his $25 investment. This means that he multiplied his capital $21,000/$25 = 840 times in three months—the interval that usually elapses between the time you mail your release and the time it appears in print.

Know the Numbers of Wealth Publicity

Cecil took out another *anything* loan to tide him over his initial promotion and manufacturing period. This loan provided cash for promotion materials and products Cecil sent out in response to the inquiries and orders he received from his first publicity effort. Naturally, he had no trouble obtaining such a loan when his business showed so much promise. Here's how I explained the numbers of wealth publicity to him.

Go to a large local library and ask the librarian for reference copies of *Standard Rate and Data* for consumer (i.e., the general public) magazines and for industrial magazines. Sit down in the library and:

1. Make a list of the name and address of every magazine you think would be interested in running your new-product release.

2. Alongside the magazine name, list the circulation; i.e., the number of subscribers given in *Standard Rate and Data*.

3. Find the total readership of all the magazines you've chosen. To do this, simply take the sum of the circulation quantity listed for each magazine on your list.

My experience shows that you need at least one million subscribers to the magazines of your choice if you are to obtain significant results. But if you wish to market test your products with fewer subscribers, go ahead and try. If you do, be extremely careful about how you interpret the results.

Evaluate the Response You Receive

Now here is the key point about this method of market testing any product or service:

You must obtain a total response of at least one-tenth of one percent of the readers of the magazines to whom you sent promotion material before you go ahead with a full-scale marketing program.

Note that the response can be either in the form of orders or inquiries for further information; i.e., add the number of orders and number of inquiries to obtain the total response. You'll receive orders for the product if you include its price in the release. Since there's nothing as exhilarating or as encouraging as receiving money in the mail, I strongly recommend that you include the price of the product or service in every release you send out.

To save you some figuring, I've computed the minimum response (orders plus inquiries) that you should receive for various total numbers of subscribers. Thus, with a one-tenth of one percent response you should receive:

TARGET MARKET TEST RESPONSE

Total Number of Subscribers	Minimum Response
1,000,000	1,000
2,000,000	2,000
3,000,000	3,000
4,000,000	4,000
5,000,000	5,000
6,000,000	6,000
8,000,000	8,000
10,000,000	10,000
12,000,000	12,000
14,000,000	14,000
16,000,000	16,000
18,000,000	18,000
20,000,000	20,000

Thus, if you send your new-product or new-service release to magazines having a total circulation of 8,000,000 readers and you receive 1,600 orders and 6,700 inquiries, the total response is $1,600 + 6,700 = 8,300$. Inspecting your Target Response Table above, you see that you need at least 8,000 responses before going ahead. Since you received 8,300 responses, you have a profitable product and you should go ahead. As a general guide, we can say that any response greater than that listed in the table means that we're in the big money, so far as our product is concerned.

How to Convert Inquiries to Orders

Many people have asked me: "How many inquiries should I be able to convert to orders for my product or service?" My answer, based on wide experience with hundreds of products and services is: You should, with well-written and neatly printed promotional material, be able to convert—sell your product to—at least 20 out of every 100 inquirers on your first response. Thus, with 6,700 inquiries as in the above case, you should be able to make $(20/100) \times 6,700 = 1,340$ sales. Since you received 1,600 orders, your total sale will be $1,600 + 1,340 = 2,940$, or nearly 3,000.

To convert inquiries to orders, take the following three steps:

(1) Send to each person inquiring about your product or service: (a) A brief description of the product or service, featuring its advantages, (b) a coupon-type order blank (c) an addressed envelope.

(2) Offer some type of incentive for ordering quickly. Typical incentives you might offer include free materials related to the product or service, a reduced price for quantity orders, etc.

(3) If you have time, follow up on those people who don't order within three weeks by sending them another mailing. Using this follow-up technique, you should be able to convert to sales a total of 25 out of every 100 inquiries you receive, as compared with 20 out of 100 when you don't use follow-up. So follow-up is really worthwhile.

The Anything Loan Is for You!

There are thousands of ways you can build your future using OPM. And the *anything* loan could be *your* way. Why not try one today and see if it is?

Collateral Loans Often Pay Off Big

Some of the words related to the borrowing of money for business or personal uses look bigger and sound more important than they really are. *Collateral* is one of those words which often frighten people who are starting to build a fortune.

Don't let any of these words frighten you. Your author, through the medium of this book, will try to answer every question you have concerning the successful borrowing and repayment of the money you need. Let's take a closer look at collateral to learn how you can use it to build your wealth.

Use Collateral to Back Your Loan

Suppose you can't find a cosigner for a loan you need? And you were turned down for business and compensating balance loans. What then? All is not lost. You can use another technique to assure the bank it will be repaid (because this, as we saw earlier, is what every bank wants). This money-generating technique uses *collateral* in place of a cosigner, compensating balance, or other guarantee of repayment.

What is collateral for a business or personal loan? *Collateral is any property or other valuable asset which can be offered as security for a loan.* If you are unable to repay your loan the lender sells your collateral for, hopefully, the amount you owe. Any excess received from the sale of your collateral would be returned to you after the payment of any interest arrears, penalties, or late charges.

What can you use as collateral? Here are typical items which are generally acceptable as collateral to most lenders:

Real estate	Stocks and bonds
Automobiles	Savings bank deposits
Jewelry	Trucks
Boat	Home
Factory	Insurance policy cash value
Farm livestock	Business machinery
Accounts receivable	Contracts for income
Valuable postage stamps	Rare coins

Talk to lenders in your area. You may find that they will accept other collateral for business and personal loans. Thus, in the oil-producing areas of the nation, bankers and lenders may accept oil properties as collateral. But you won't learn what is acceptable to your local lenders until you ask. So start now—if a collateral loan interests you.

How to Use Collateral

When a bank or other lender tells you that you need a cosigner or another form of guarantee on your loan, ask the loan officer: "Could I substitute collateral for a cosigner?"

"What kind of collateral do you have?" he'll ask.

Answer this question carefully. Take my advice and:

Mention only the collateral you think will be acceptable and which you are willing to put up for the loan. Don't waste your collateral— you may need it for a future loan.

Collateral, like any other valuable asset, should be conserved. So don't blab out a list of all your collateral because the lender will ask that you pledge the most desirable. Let's look at Mr. BWB (Beginning Wealth Builder) again to see how this works.

Don't Waste Collateral Borrowing Power

Mr. BWB has, when he walks into the bank, the following collateral:
(a) An auto having a "Red Book" value of $2,000
(b) Thirty shares of stock worth $100 per share
(c) Two lots of land worth $1,000 each.

Mr. BWB applies for a $2,000 personal loan. He fills out the loan application. The banker, after studying the application, says "Your salary isn't large enough to cover this loan, Mr. BWB. You'll need a co-signer."

"How about my collateral?" Mr. BWB asks. "I have a brand new car that is fully paid for, thirty shares of XYZ stock, and two lots of land in a fast-growing industrial area."

The banker ponders a few moments and says: "We'll accept *all* your collateral, Mr. BWB. That way you'll be sure to get the money you need."

Poor Mr. BWB! He's so anxious to get the money that he foolishly puts up *all* his collateral when any one of the items—his auto, stocks, or land—would have served as collateral for this loan. This incident points up an important principle of collateral loans—

Don't waste your collateral. Put up only enough collateral to cover the loan—no more. Save as much collateral as possible for future loans.

Know How Collateral Is Figured

Bankers will seldom allow, for collateral purposes, the amount you paid for an item unless the item has increased enormously in value while you owned it. And any money you may presently owe on an item will be deducted from the allowed collateral value before the final collateral allowance is fixed by the bank. Let's see how this works.

Stocks and Bonds

The bank or other lender will usually allow you 70 percent of the current market price of the stocks or bonds when you offer them as collateral. Thus, if you own a share of XYZ stock which has a current market price of $100, the bank would allow you to borrow 0.70 ($100) = $70 on each share you put up for collateral.

Mr. BWB has 30 shares of this stock; hence he could borrow $70 (30 shares) = $2,100. Since he needed only $2,000 in the above situation, his 30 shares would easily cover his loan.

When you use stocks or bonds as collateral for a loan you must leave the stock certificates in the hands of the bank until the loan is paid off. You must also sign a certificate of hypothecation which is a document permitting the bank to sell your stocks or bonds if you fail to repay the loan.

AUTOS, TRUCKS, BOATS, ETC.

Autos and trucks used as collateral for loans are often evaluated by lenders by means of the *American Auto Appraisal Book* published by American Auto Appraisers, 194 Grove Avenue, Detroit, Mich. 48203. Boats are evaluated by using the *BUC Directory*, published by BUC International Corp., 2455 E. Sunrise Blvd., Ft. Lauderdale, Fla. 33304.

The *book value* is the present value of an auto, truck, boat, or any similar item, stated in a recognized and respected appraisal book. The lender will usually grant you a loan up to the book value of the item.

Let's say you have a one-year-old car with a book value of $3,000. You can borrow any amount of money up to $3,000 using the car as collateral, if the car is fully paid for. If you still owe money on the car—say $1,000—then you can borrow the difference between this amount and the book value, or $3,000 − 1,000 = $2,000. The same is true of trucks, boats, airplanes, etc.

OTHER FORMS OF COLLATERAL

Some of the best forms of collateral are paper—a will, a deed, a contract. Of the three the contract is probably the most powerful. So we'll take a quick look at contracts to see how you can use them in your wealth building.

Use Jet-Age Borrowing Techniques

Let's say you're interested in opening a trucking business. But you don't have the cash needed to get started. This is a familiar problem to many BWBs.

While you're looking into the various opportunities in the trucking business you hear of a company that wants to hire trucks for three years. You go to the company and ask to see the transportation manager. "Sir," you say, "I'll lease you the trucks you need and I'll save you money."

He's immediately interested. After a period of negotiation, the transportation manager agrees to give you a contract whereby his firm will lease ten trucks from you for three years.

You then go to your local bank and say to the loan officer: "ABC Company will give me a contract to lease ten trucks for three years at $100 per month per truck. How much can I borrow using the contract as collateral?"

The loan officer ponders for a few minutes. "Your contract will give you a total income of $36,000 in three years. What will you do with this income?"

"I'll use it to pay for the trucks I intend to lease to the ABC Company."

"Hmm," the loan officer says. "This loan has *real* possibilities. You have the leasing income which can serve as collateral. But you'll also have the trucks which can serve as collateral too! We'll be delighted to lend you as much as you need, Mr. BWB."

You negotiate a loan for $20,000 for a three-year period. Taking $10,000, you make a $1,000 down payment on each of ten trucks. You hold the other $10,000 as operating funds to take care of expenses that may arise during the first few months you're in business. Thus, using jet-age financing, you've moved from little or no business to a full-fledged operating company with money in the bank and solid assets (your trucks) earning income for you every day of the week.

How You Can Get Contracts

"That's a nice arrangement you just described," you say. "But I have no interest at all in the trucking business. How can I get contracts I can use as collateral?"

You *can* get contracts if you take these six steps:

(1) Decide what business you'd like to be in
(2) Check the need for your business
(3) Find out what you could charge customers
(4) Look into contract possibilities
(5) Form a company if business prospects are good
(6) Go out and sell your contracts

When you take the first four of these steps you'll probably find that your greatest chances for contracts are in the area of service. Thus, large and small firms often sign contracts for:

- Equipment rental
- Building cleaning
- Machinery maintenance
- Publication printing
- Office or factory space rental
- Consulting staffs

There are many other types of service you can sell on a contract basis to important firms. Just look into your own past for unique experiences and knowledge which you "rent out" at profitable fees.

Use This Supersonic Money Secret

Most BWBs don't recognize the value of a contract because they haven't yet thought through the matter. Once they do, though, they realize how valuable a contract can be in their search for wealth.

Also, many BWBs sense an important supersonic money secret related to contracts. This secret is:

You can pyramid contracts; i.e., use the income from one contract to obtain a business leading to another contract. And pyramiding is the key to greater wealth sooner.

This important principle is used by wealth builders everywhere. The way to the big money for you, for me, for everyone, is through the action-fed growth of whatever income and capital we have.

Accentuate the Positive

Recognize—here and now—that a small income from your own business is a valuable asset for borrowing purposes. Why? Because you can accentuate your future growth possibilities when you apply for a loan.

Instead of crying about your small current income, you accentuate the positive; i.e., you talk about your big future income. This approach has two valuable features:

1. *The loan officer is led (by you) to think in big-money terms.* Instead of sizing you up as a "2,000 dollar loan" he sees you as a "25,000 dollar loan." Certainly, it's easier to negotiate with a loan officer who sees you as a big prospect than it is with one who sees you as not worth his time.

2. *Thinking in big-money terms brings big money to you.* I am firmly convinced—based on my personal experience, and the experiences of thousands of other wealth builders who become millionaires starting with no capital of their own—that if you think big money you'll make big money. This is a wealth principle that many lazy people scoff at. Yet it works—anywhere, for anyone.

Think Big—Think Rich

You *can* get contracts that are valuable for collateral purposes. But you stand little chance if you think in small, negative terms. You must think BIG—think RICH.

While contracts can provide the collateral you need to start thinking big and thinking rich, property deeds, mentioned earlier, may allow you to think your way to great wealth in just a few months. Let's see how you can use property deeds to put you in the big money.

Get Rich on Trust Deeds

Almost every big fortune ever built anywhere in this world eventually deals in real estate. Many fortunes begin with, and stay with, real estate. Why is there this great interest in real estate? There are several reasons, but the most important is *leverage.*

Leverage has a simple meaning in real estate. It means that:

In real estate a small amount of capital can control property valued at a large amount of money. Earnings from the property can (*a*) pay for the property and any financing required to control it, and (*b*) pay the owner an income.

Expressed in numbers, the leverage obtainable through using property deeds as collateral for one or more loans can give you an income of $1,000 for every $100 you invest. Thus, your leverage is $1,000/$100 = 10 to 1.

Sometimes you can obtain infinite leverage; that is, you can become sole owner of a desirable building with *no* cash investment of any kind. Further, you may "mortgage out" of the deal or:

Mortgaging out gives you ownership of a property with no money down and with a cash payment to you.

Mortgaging out is the ultimate in collateral loans using property deeds. Let's see how you can put this important principle to work for yourself —if real estate interests you. And it should because you can hardly expect to think big and think rich unless you're willing to consider *every* possible way you might build a great fortune.

How to Borrow for Property and Cash

Let's say that a $500,000 property interests you. In fact, you can't sleep, relax, or eat, thinking about this property. Why? Because it's a modern 50-unit apartment building which has a total rental income of $100,000 per year when fully rented. Here's how the financial statement for this building looks:

Building price	$ 500,000
Bank mortgage	−400,000
Cash you need	$ 100,000
Second mortgage available	125,000
Net cash to you	$ 25,000

Let's look at this statement for a moment. The bank mortgage on this building is 80 percent of the building price; i.e., 0.8 ($500,000) = $400,000. Most banks will readily lend this amount on a building in good condition. On a Federal Housing Administration (FHA) backed loan, a bank will lend you up to 90 percent of the building price.

The second mortgage of $125,000 is usually granted by an insurance company, a real-estate finance company, or some other organization—generally not a bank. The building serves as your collateral for both the first and second mortgage loans.

"Why," you intelligently ask, "do I have to borrow $125,000 for the second mortgage when only $100,000 is needed?"

You don't *have* to borrow more than you need. But this building is an excellent example of an important collateral loan and real-estate principle:

When you have good collateral in any real estate—such as a building—borrow as much as you can on it for the longest term possible —while the lender is interested and willing.

Why shouldn't you "walk away" with $25,000, or more, tax-free income if you're smart enough to work a good business deal? Plenty of others do it every day and never have another money worry because the property they use for collateral pays off the loan which puts tax-free cash in their pocket *and*, at the same time, gives them a profitable income! Let's see how.

Earn Big Money Every Month

The annual rental income from this building, allowing a 5 percent loss for vacancies, is $95,000. Your operating expenses for heat, light, water, labor, maintenance, etc., will probably be 40 percent of the rental income, or 0.4 ($95,000) = $38,000. This leaves $95,000 − 38,000 = $57,000 per year as operating income.

From your operating income you must pay off your first and second mortgages. The first-mortgage payment will be $28,000 per year, in cluding interest, while the second-mortgage payment will be $15,000 per year for about 15 years. Your net money-in-fist (MIF) is therefore $57,000 — 28,000 — 15,000 = $14,000 per year, or more than $1,000 per month.

"But that's not *real* money," you sniff. "What I want is the big income —$100,000 per year, or more!"

True, $14,000 per year isn't really big money. But you also have $25,000 tax-free money in your hand, making your first-year income $25,000 + $14,000 = $39,000. Now we're getting somewhere. Further, if you plan your taxes wisely, the $14,000 rental income will also be tax-free. If your family status put you in the 30 percent tax bracket, your $39,000 tax-free income during the first year equals a taxable income of nearly $51,000. More interesting?

Use Your Financial Ingenuity

But we're not finished yet. Let's say you use a seven-year *standing* or *balloon* second mortgage. With this arrangement you pay only the interest due on the second mortgage for 83 months. At the start of the eighty-fourth month you pay off the principal due on the second mort- gage, or $125,000. This arrangement raises your MIF but costs you more in interest. However, the interest you pay is tax deductible.

The interest on your second mortgage would be about $7,000 per year. Thus, your MIF income would rise by about $8,000 per year because the payment on the second mortgage discussed above was $15,000. Hence, your annual cash income with a standing second mortgage would be $22,000. Your first-year income would be $22,000 + $25,000 = $47,000.

Pyramid Your Way to a Million-Dollar Income

You don't have to stop with just one building. The technique that works for this building will work for any other. Keep in mind the fact that:

Collateral loans are always attractive to lenders. You'll seldom be turned down when you apply for a loan backed by first-class col- lateral.

Let's say you decide that you'd like to own 50 buildings, each of which gives you a MIF income of more than $20,000 per year. Does the idea of 50 buildings sound awesome? It needn't. Plenty of real-estate operators own more than 50 buildings. And they're the most relaxed business people you'll ever meet. Many of them winter in the Caribbean, summer in Europe. In between they casually inspect their properties.

With 50 buildings of the type we're analyzing, your yearly income would be 50 ($22,000) = $1,100,000. If you had only half this number of buildings, or 25, your annual income would be $550,000, Meanwhile, of course, you're increasing your equity (your ownership) in each of these properties. Should you decide to sell any or all of your properties, you will earn a neat profit at the lower capital-gains tax rates.

You Can Make Your Fortune Today

I've just shown you how to net a million dollars per year using other people's money. Further, you will pick up an extra $25,000 in cash on each income property you buy, when you borrow the money to pay for the property.

"But I'll have to pay interest on all the money I borrow," you say.

Certainly you will! But your properties will be paying the interest for you out of their earnings. And the interest is tax deductible. To calm any BWB's fear about paying interest on borrowed money I always ask him just one question:

Which would you rather do—pay interest on loans on which you net up to $1 million per year, or pay no interest and have a yearly income of zero dollars?

The answer is, as I'm almost sure your answer is, "Pay the interest!" This answer is almost in the same vein as, I hope, your answer to a similar question: "Which would you rather have—a large income on which you pay high income taxes or a low income on which you pay little or no tax?" As one BWB says: "Give me the large income *now;* I'll worry about high taxes later!"

What's more—if you earn $100,000 a year in your own business you'll have a lot more after-tax dollars left in your pocket than if you earn the same amount in salary. Why? Because in your own business you're entitled to many more deductions than when your only income is from salary.

Build Stock Wealth on Collateral

Some BWBs prefer the stock and bond markets as a source of income. Great! Just as long as you recognize the risks in stock and bond investments, I'm delighted to show you how to earn more money using OPM. While there are some restrictions to borrowing money to buy stocks or bonds, let's first look at the leverage you can obtain using stocks or bonds as collateral.

When dealing with banks on stock loans you'll frequently hear the word *margin*. The margin is the amount of money you must put up to buy stock using borrowed funds. Thus, if a 70 percent margin is required, you must put up $70 cash for every $100 worth of stock you buy. And, conversely, a bank or other lender will lend you $70 for every $100 worth of stock you put up as collateral. Let's put margin to work for you right now!

Margin Leverage Fortune Miracles

Let's say you have $10,000 in borrowed money. You obtained this money by means of a personal loan, a collateral loan, a business loan, or any other type of loan. (We'll discuss the extra type of loan later.)

You want to use the money to buy stock. Your analysis of the market indicates that the stock you're planning to buy will, hopefully, go up in price. Hence, you want to buy as many shares as possible. Here's what you do.

To obtain the largest number of shares of stock using the stock itself as collateral, take out a series of loans.

Let's say that the stock you want to buy in XYZ Company is selling at $100 per share. Neglecting the broker's fee, which is small, you could buy $10,000/100 = 100 shares of XYZ using the borrowed money you have. Now follow this 12-step procedure:

1. Buy 100 shares of XYZ at $100 each.
2. Use the 100 shares as collateral for a $7,000 loan, i.e., 70 percent of the market value of your shares.
3. Buy 70 shares of XYZ stock with the borrowed $7,000.
4. Use the 70 shares as collateral for a $4,900 loan; i.e., 70 percent of the market value of these shares.
5. Buy 49 shares of XYZ stock with the borrowed $4,900.
6. Use the 49 shares as collateral for a $3,400 loan.

7. Buy 34 shares of XYZ stock with the borrowed $3,400.
8. Use the 34 shares as collateral for a $2,200 loan.
9. Buy 22 shares of XYZ.
10. Borrow $1,400 on the 22 shares.
11. Buy 14 shares of XYZ,
12. Borrow $1,000 on the 14 shares. Hold the cash.

You now own $100 + 70 + 49 + 34 + 22 + 14 = 289$ shares of XYZ stock at $100 per share. Thus, your shares are worth $100 (289) = $28,900. Yet you paid only $9,000 for these shares, excluding brokerage fees. This means you have leveraged yourself by: $28,900/$9,000 = 3.21 times. This is the *margin leverage* that produces fortunes miraculously. Note that you also have $1,000 in cash, or you could have 22 more shares if you invested this $1,000 cash in XYZ stock.

Ride Your Leverage to Enormous Wealth

Let's watch your XYZ stock closely. While XYZ is not exactly a purely speculative stock, it is one of the go-go high flyers. As such, your stock rises from $100 to $175 per share during a seven-month period. (This is not at all unusual for any of the high flyers—computer, electronics, office equipment, hospital supply, and similar stocks.)

At $175 per share your 289 shares are worth $175 (289) = $50,575. This means you made a gross profit of $50,575 − $9,000 = $41,575 in seven months without investing one cent of your own! Commissions and interest would run about $1,500. Thus, you'd net out with a profit of about $40,075. Not bad for a guy who hardly had a bank account seven months ago. If you could do this twice a year (as many others have) you could net more than $80,000 per year on OPM. (And, of course, you could raise your income if you put *all* your borrowed cash into stock.)

The Key to OPM Leverage

Is all of this a pipe dream? No! It certainly is not. But you must have the key that opens the lock to using OPM collateral loans. Here's the key.

Banks are not receptive to people wanting to borrow money to invest in stocks using other stock as collateral. Hence, you must have another use in mind when you apply for a collateral loan which uses stock for collateral.

Once again, as we mentioned in Chapter 2, you must use your ingenuity when building a fortune on OPM. If you feel you'd prefer not to change your mind about the use you'll make of borrowed money, then explore the more conventional loans we discuss elsewhere in this book.

Remember—*there is nothing illegal about changing your mind as to the use you'll make of borrowed money.* Keep this in mind when planning your fortune building.

Use Your Imagination

You now have the facts you need to start a wealth-building program using OPM obtained through collateral loans. While I've given you the highlights, I'm sure you can work out many variations of these techniques. Why? Because

You can THINK yourself rich! The more time you spend trying to devise ways to get rich, the greater your chances. So start thinking —NOW!

You'll also find that the practices and requirements of lenders will vary from one city or state to another, and from one economic period to another. Hence, you have to do some thinking on your own to determine how you can best meet the lender's requirements.

But keep one fact in mind at all times when considering a collateral loan. This key fact, which can give you greater confidence when dealing with any lender, is:

Lenders, in general, like to make collateral loans. So you can apply for your loan with confidence. Knowing this, you improve your chances for acceptance.

A collateral loan can put you on your way to great wealth. Check into the collateral loan sources in your area today. You may find more money looking for a "home" than you ever thought existed!

8

How State and Local Loans
Can Build Your Wealth

You may not realize it but you could, at this very moment, be sitting on a million dollars, or more! "That's impossible!" you shout. "How could anyone in his right mind be sitting on a million dollars or more and not realize it? To do this a man or woman would have to be completely out of touch with life!

There's Money All Around You

Yes, I say, many people—not you, of course—are out of touch with the *money* facts of life. They are unaware that:

Most of the states, and many counties, cities, and towns, offer long-term low-interest business loans to anyone in their area who needs money to start, improve, or expand a business that offers jobs to people.

Typical loans you might obtain from local sources are:

- 100% financing of new factories
- 100% financing of new production machines
- 100% financing of factory expansion
- 100% financing of business real estate
- 100% financing of job-training programs

"Are you sure about this?" you ask. "One hundred percent financing of my factory? That means I don't have to put up a dime!"

That's right. Not only am I sure of this, but later in this chapter I'll give you the name and address of the agency which makes such loans in your state. This list alone could be worth millions of dollars to you.

States Need Business

Many states have a group called the State Development Commission. The main purpose of such a commission is to bring new business and new jobs into the state. There are several ways of doing this:

- Attracting out-of-state firms
- Helping expand existing in-state firms
- Assisting the start of new in-state firms
- Financing job-training activities

While most state commissions give attention to all four of these activities, the last three receive the most attention. Why? Because wooing out-of-state firms is a wild, competitive gamble with almost every state trying to win a few choice firms.

So in recent years, many states have concentrated on building up the business of existing or new in-state firms. "Is this good or bad for my lending needs?" you ask. It's good; in fact, it's great! Your state wants you to build your business so that it creates more jobs for state residents.

Get in on State Generosity

To induce you to expand, build, or start a profitable business, many states offer:

- Full real estate financing
- Full building construction financing
- Full business equipment financing
- Tax-free business periods for up to 10 years
- Funds for miscellaneous business expansion
- Special bonds to finance your business
- Educational facilities for personnel training
- Manpower assistance for your business

These, and other aids, can get your business moving and put big money in your pocket. Every state wants a piece of the business action; i.e., the state wants growing, prosperous businesses within its borders. So if you have a good idea for starting or expanding a business, see the state development commission listed later in this chapter. You'll find that the welcome mat is always ready for you.

Recognize the Size of State Aid

Some BWBs reject the idea of state aid because they think the amount of money they can obtain is "peanuts." Perhaps the amount is insignificant to some people but it isn't to me, and I hope you feel the same way. "But how can I feel the same way if I don't know the amount I can obtain?" you ask.

Great! That's exactly how a businessman should think. To answer your question, typical state aid to businesses ranges between:

$$\$15,000 \text{ and } \$15,000,000$$

with most loans in the range of:

$$\$300,000 \text{ to } \$3,000,000$$

Now, good friends, among my many activities I am an executive in a $350-million-per-year corporation. This corporation is in a respectable position on *Fortune* magazine's annual list of America's 500 largest corporations. Yet in this corporation we actively chase a $300,000 piece of business. And we literally run after a $3 million piece of business!

So when I see a BWB turn his back on state aid as being too small for him, I lose interest in helping him. Why? Because he's out of touch with the financial facts of life and there's little that can be done for him. Inflation may be reducing the value of the dollar, but any sum of money greater than $10,000 is still a powerful piece of change in the hands of an ambitious BWB.

How to Get State or Local Business Aid

To achieve the greatest success when you apply for state or local business aid:

(1) Decide how much money you need
(2) Select the major purpose for the money
(3) Write a brief statement of why you need the money
(4) Figure how many jobs the loan will provide
(5) Compute the profit your firm will earn

Carefully review your facts and figures. Imagine yourself sitting in the state or local business aid office, presenting your aid story. If you can, try to have a friend listen to your story while you present it. Ask him to criticize your facts; tell him to ask questions which probe your story and the reasons you give for needing the money.

Why do I recommend this dry-run approach to state and local aid? Because I want you to obtain the money you need. When you apply the dry-run method you quickly spot any "holes" in your story. Once you know what these holes are you can easily patch them.

Winning Ways Are Easy to Learn

Take the case of Dick B., who wanted to borrow $500,000 from his state to convert some waterfront property into a marina. Dick called me at home to ask if I would be willing to advise him. I said I'd be delighted.

We met for lunch at a time that was convenient to Dick. As soon as we were seated, he launched into his story.

"I have my eye on a piece of waterfront land which I can get for no money down, if I can get a loan to build a marina on the property," Dick said.

"Sounds like you can't lose," I said. "But I'd like to ask you a few questions about the whole idea before we go any further. The questions may be a trifle personal, so please don't be offended. I'm not trying to pry into your life, but I do want to be sure I can help you." "Fire away," Dick said with a laugh.

The questions I asked Dick were the same ones I thought a state business aid examiner might ask. They were:

(1) Why do you want to build a marina on this property?
(2) What will the state gain from this project?
(3) How soon could you repay a loan we might make to you?

Dick's answers were most interesting. As a test of your own feeling for these matters, mark after each answer, in the space provided below, a yes or no, indicating whether the state aid examiner would accept it as a valid reason for granting a loan. Here are Dick's answers.

(1) Marinas interest me. I've always wanted to be in the marina business and this is a good spot for such a business. _____ Yes; _____ No.
(2) The state will have vacant property converted to business property. Hence, higher taxes will be paid to the state. _____ Yes; _____ No.
(3) For the amount of money I need, at least 10 years would be required to repay the state. _____ Yes; _____ No.

What is your opinion of these answers? My opinion was: (1) — No; (2) — Yes; (3) — Yes. Check your opinion against mine. Then I'll explain my reasoning.

You Must See the Whole Picture

The people running the financial office of any state aid group are interested in helping the *state* first, and *you* second. So when you approach your state for a business loan, you must see the whole picture; i.e., the state's outlook as well as your own. Now let's review Dick's answers.

Dick's answer to Question 1 sees only one side of the situation—his side. No state in the union will lend a businessman money just because a certain business interests him. To overcome this situation we changed Dick's answer to that shown below.

The answer Dick gave to Question 2 is fair—he could get by with it because the state's viewpoint, higher taxes, is featured. But the answer could be improved somewhat, as you'll see later.

The same goes for Question 3. Ten years is a relatively short payoff period for a state loan. Why? Some states allow as long as 30 years for business loan payoffs.

Aim Your Loan Application at Success

I worked with Dick to improve his answers to the three questions. Here are the revised answers.

1. A marina will improve the land being considered and will beautify the area in question, which is presently run down. Further, the marina will provide employment for at least 12 people in the area. At this time there is no industry on the land, yet there are a number of employable persons in nearby homes.
2. Higher land, business, and employment taxes will be paid the state by the marina on the improved land, marina income, and employees' earnings. Thus, a non-productive area will be turned into a revenue generator for the state.
3. The loan required ($500,000) could be paid off in 10 years at the rate of $50,000 per year, plus interest, if the state desired. Should the state prefer a longer payoff period, the borrower would be willing to agree to a 15- to 30-year payoff period.

State Funds Build a Fortune

Dick got his loan and invested the money in the marina. That was about two years ago. Today his marina is a booming business. He has offered the state to pay off the loan sooner but the state declined. "Invest your surplus cash in another business," the state agent told Dick. "And if you need more money—say a million or so—just see us."

Meanwhile, the town and county officials in Dick's area are banging on his front door. "Please take a loan from us," each says. "We have money we want to put to work. And you've proven you're reliable and a shrewd businessman. That property lay vacant for years and nobody saw its potential."

"How much is Dick taking out of the business?" you ask. "He's probably just making ends meet!"

If you call $100,000 a year just "making ends meet," then Dick is just getting by. But if you think that kind of an income is a good start towards a fortune on OPM, then Dick is doing nicely.

What's more, Dick is building his equity in the business; that is, each year he owns more of the business as he pays off the loan. In a few years he'll have a highly saleable business which he can sell and pay taxes on his profit at the low capital-gains rate. What more can we ask for when we're investing only time and energy—and other people's money? This is truly a dream come true—building your own future at no expense to yourself.

Train Your Workers Using State Funds

Most states want a supply of skilled labor within their borders because this attracts industry. To build their skilled-worker supply, many states lend money to industry for training purposes. Thus, if you have people whose skills you want to upgrade, you may be in a good position to get a hefty loan from your state.

Now here is a key wealth-building secret for every business that wants to train workers. This is the first time that this secret has ever been published anywhere, yet knowledge of it has helped make some people millionaires. The secret is this:

> State funds for training can be used for teachers' salaries, teaching aids, and training equipment. Select training equipment that can also be used for production—then you'll be financed to buy the machines that will make your product.

Put the Five Ms to Work

Many businessmen think of their business in terms of the five Ms of industry:

● Men   ● Money   ● Markets   ● Machines   ● Materials

When you use state aid to train your workers you put four of these Ms to work using OPM. The four you put to work are: Men (by your training); Money (which you borrow); Machines (which you buy with borrowed money); Materials (your men work on while training). All you need now is Markets—and your state may help you with these by finding customers for you.

Ted E. borrowed $200,000 from his state to build an auto repair center. As soon as the center was half finished, Ted began advertising for auto mechanics. To his shock, and the state's, Ted didn't have one answer to his ads. Ted faced the prospect of opening a shiny new auto diagnostic and repair center without a single mechanic on hand. What could he do?

There was only one answer—Ted would have to train his own mechanics. But this takes money. And Ted didn't have any extra cash because his $200,000 loan from the state was just enough to cover his investment in equipment and operating expenses for the first three months.

So Ted put another wealth secret to work, even though he didn't realize this until later. He went back to the state industrial development bureau and asked for *another* loan—this one to finance the machines and training of his mechanics. He received approval of the loan application within two days. Why? Because:

State agencies are ready to lend more money when the repayment of their first loan is endangered by a lack of skilled personnel.

Ted sensed this. So he included the cost of another diagnostic machine when he applied for the training loan. This doubled the capacity of his service center, while giving him the machine he needed to train his mechanics.

Today Ted's auto service center is booming—thanks to OPM which provided the Men, Money, Materials, and Machines he needed.

Get Local Funds, Too

Here's another "state secret" you ought to know because it can put real money—$100,000 or more—in your pocket. This secret is:

It's much easier to borrow additional funds from your county or city once your state has granted you a loan.

Why is this so? Because many local business-aid agencies are relatively unsophisticated. They think this way:

If the state granted this firm a big loan, or a small loan, the firm must be reliable and reputable. So why shouldn't we approve another loan?

When such reasoning occurs—and it occurs again and again—you may find that you have, as they say, "money running out of your ears." Then your problem will be one of finding ways in which you can put all that money to work earning a profit for your company.

So don't overlook the double payoff, or even the triple payoff, that may be available to you through:

- State business loans
- County development loans
- City business loans

There's more money waiting to be picked up from various business agencies than you ever thought existed.

Where to Get Your State Money

Here's a list of the business loan agencies for certain states, territories, etc. To apply for a loan, simply call (you'll find the telephone number in the following list or in a large city phone book), or write the agency in your state, requesting a loan application. They'll send the application within a few days.

Important Notice

Some state business loan agencies lend *only* to established businesses or *only* to out-of-state businesses they are trying to attract. So don't be discouraged if you're told that loans are unavailable to new or yet-to-be established businesses. Just try another loan source—such as a bank, financing company, private lender, etc.

STATE BUSINESS AID AGENCIES

Alabama Planning and Industrial Development Board
State Office Building
Montgomery, Ala.
205-265-2341

Alaska Department of Economic Development and Planning
Division of Industrial Development
Box 1421
Juneau, Alaska

Arizona Development Board
1500 West Jefferson Street
Phoenix, Ariz. 85007
602-271-4431

Arkansas Industrial Development Commission
205 State Capitol
Little Rock, Ark. 72203
501-376-1961

California Department of Finance
State Capitol Building
Sacramento, Calif. 95814
915-445-9862

Connecticut Development Commission
State Office Building
Hartford, Conn. 06115
203-527-6341

Delaware State Development Department
45, The Green
Dover, Del. 19901

Florida Development Commission
Industrial Division
Talahassee, Fla. 32304
305-224-1215

Georgia Department of Industry and Trade
100 State Capitol
Atlanta, Ga.
404-523-1706

Hawaii Department of Planning and Economic Development
426 Queen St.
Honolulu, Hawaii 96813

Idaho Department of Commerce and Development
State House
Boise, Idaho 83701
208-344-5811

Illinois Board of Economic Development
400 State Office Building
Springfield, Ill. 62706

Indiana Department of Commerce
336 State House
Indianapolis, Ind. 46201
317-633-4450

Iowa Development Commission
250 Jewett Building
Des Moines, Ia. 50309
515-282-0231

Kansas Department of Economic Development
State Office Building
Topeka, Kan.
913-235-0011

Kentucky Department of Commerce
Frankfort, Ky.
502-227-9661

Louisiana Department of Commerce and Industry
Baton Rouge, La. 70804
504-342-7733

Maine Department of Economic Development
Augusta, Me. 04330
State House
207-623-4511

Maryland Department of Economic Development
State Office Building
Annapolis, Md.
301-268-3371

Massachusetts Department of Commerce and Development
100 Cambridge St.
Boston, Mass. 02202
617-727-3218

Michigan Department of Economic Expansion
Steven T. Mason Building
Lansing, Mich. 48926
517-373-3530

Minnesota Department of Business Development
160 State Office Building
St. Paul, Minn. 55101
612-221-2755

Mississippi Agricultural and Industrial Board
1504 State Office Building
Jackson, Miss.
601-355-9361

Missouri Division of Commerce and Industrial Development
Jefferson Building
Jefferson City, Mo. 65102
314-636-7185

Montana State Planning Board
Mitchell Building
Helena, Mont. 59601
406-442-3260

Nebraska Division of Resources
1107 State Capitol
Lincoln, Neb. 68509
402-477-8984

Nevada Department of Economic Development
Carson City, Nev. 89701
702-882-7478

New Hampshire Division of Economic Development
State House Annex
Concord, N. H. 03301
603-225-6611

New Jersey Division of Economic Development
Department of Conservation and Economic Development
Trenton, N.J. 08625
609-292-2733

New York Bureau of Industrial Development
Department of Commerce
Albany, N.Y.
518-474-3777

North Carolina Commerce and Industry Division
Department of Conservation and Development
Raleigh, N.C.
919-834-3611

North Dakota Economic Development Commission
State Capitol
Bismark, N.D. 58501
701-223-8000

Ohio Development Department
1005 Ohio Department Building
Columbus, Ohio 43215
614-469-2480

Oklahoma Department of Commerce and Industry
P.O. Box 3327, Capitol Station
Oklahoma City, Okla. 73105
405-525-6541

Oregon Department of Commerce
Division of Planning and Development
560 State Office Building
Portland, Ore. 97201
503-226-2161

Pennsylvania Bureau of Industrial Development
Department of Commerce
Harrisburg, Pa. 17120
717-787-6620

Rhode Island Industrial Building Authority
Roger Williams Building
Providence, R.I. 02908
401-521-7100

South Carolina State Development Board
Columbus, S.C.
893-765-2912

South Dakota Industrial Development Expansion Agency
State Office Building
Pierre, S.D.
605-224-5911

Tennessee Division for Industrial Development
Cordell Hull Building
Nashville, Tenn. 37219
615-371-2549

Texas Industrial Commission
Sam Houston State Office Building
Austin, Texas
512-475-4331

Utah Industrial and Employment Planning
174 Social Hall Ave.
Salt Lake City, Utah 84110
801-322-1433

Vermont Development Department
Industrial Division
Montpelier, Vt. 05602
802-233-2311

Washington Department of Commerce and Economic Development
Industrial Development Division
General Administration Building
Olympia, Wash. 98502
206-753-5630

West Virginia Industrial Development Division
State Capitol
Charleston, W. Va.
304-343-4411

Wisconsin Department of Resource Development
Division of Economic Development
Madison, Wis. 53702
608-266-3221

Wyoming Natural Resource Board
Supreme Court Building
Cheyenne, Wy. 82001
307-634-2711

• • • • •

Economic Development Administration
Commonwealth of Puerto Rico
P. O. Box 2672
San Juan, P. R. 00903

Use These Three Magic Wealth Builders

In this chapter, I've revealed to you a number of valuable inside
wealth secrets. Because I'm so determined to help make you wealthy,
I want to tell you about three more magic wealth builders which you
might wish to use in conjunction with a state or local loan. These three
major wealth builders are:

- Leverage
- Synergy
- Serendipity

Any one, or a combination of two or more, of these magic wealth
builders could make your fortune for you within a year or two. Let's take
a look at each of these powerful wealth builders to see how you can
put them to work earning *your* fortune.

Leverage Multiplies Your Capital

Let's say you have a $10,000 state loan to invest in a piece of real
estate, part of which you'll use for your business. You plan to hold the
remainder of the land for speculative purposes; i.e., you hope the land
will increase in value so you can sell it at a profit.

After shopping around you find that you can get a good piece of
business property free and clear for a total payment of $5,000. Thus,
you'll have $5,000 left from your $10,000 loan to invest in other speculative land or buildings—if you buy this property. You decide to buy
this land to use just for your business. You then look around for speculative land.

Talking further with your real-estate broker, you learn that you can
buy an adjacent piece of land priced at $25,000 for only 20 percent down.
This means that you can control this $25,000 worth of speculative prop-
erty with only 0.20 ($25,000) = $5,000. Thus, we can say:

Leverage permits you to control a large investment with only a small amount of cash.

You buy the speculative property using the $5,000 of OPM which you obtained from the state loan. Within a year, you receive an offer of $32,000 for the property. During the year you've paid $2,000 more on the property for taxes, mortgage interest, and mortgage principal, making your total investment $7,000. Let's see what your profit is.

When you sell the property you receive $32,000. But you still owe $18,000 on the property, i.e. $25,000 — $7,000 = $18,000. Using the money you receive on the sale, you pay off the mortgage and have $32,000 — $18,000 = $14,000 left. Thus, you've earned a $14,000 profit on a $7,000 investment. This is a profit of $14,000 (100)/$7,000 = 200 percent. (The 100 in this format converts the result to a percentage.) Any time you can make a 200 percent profit on a business deal you know that you have a magic wealth-building system working for you. So always remember:

Leverage allows you to get more mileage from your money. And, the greater your leverage, the larger your profit potential.

Be Wary of Leverage Risks

Leverage, of course, has its risks. Why? Because as you increase your leverage you go further out on the limb of risk. And, as we all know, the limb gets thinner and weaker as we approach its end. But as beginning wealth builders we must be willing to take greater risks because:

As risks increase, so do profit potentials. When we're just starting to build a fortune, we must take greater risks than when we have it made.

Never be afraid to take a business risk. What you should be afraid of is being afraid to take a business risk! As successful wealth builders say: "We have nothing to fear except fear itself."

Synergy Gives You GO POWER

Synergy is building fortunes all over the world. I see its effects everywhere I go—from Los Angeles to Dallas to Phoenix to New York; from London to Paris to Berlin to Tokyo.

What is synergy? It's a proven business principle that states:

The whole is stronger than the sum of all of its parts; i.e., two firms that merge become one firm that is stronger, and has a greater chance of success, than the two firms alone.

Let's see how this principle might work in your life to build a great fortune for you.

You, we'll say, are interested in getting into your own business. After reading this book, or any of my other three fortune-building books,* you decide to buy a girl's ballet dancing school. Why do you buy such a school? Well, you learn, from reading these books, that an ideal business for a beginner is one which:

- Is simple to run
- Doesn't need a large inventory
- Has no complex machines

- Doesn't require a large labor force
- Can be operated in a rented space
- Is easy to advertise
- Gives you an immediate cash income

A girls' ballet school is just such a business. It meets all these suggestions, plus a few more. Let's see how. Ballet schools:

- Need only one or two part-time teachers
- Require *no* inventory
- Use *no* machines
- Can be run by one or two people
- Are usually operated in a rented store
- Can be advertised cheaply, easily
- Provide a weekly cash income to you

You buy this school with $3,000 obtained as part of a $20,000 state loan. Even though you're not a ballet dancer yourself, you hire two young women ballet teachers who agree to teach three hours per day, five days a week. You advertise in small local school and religious

---

* *How to Build a Second Income Fortune in Your Spare Time, Smart Money Shortcuts to Becoming Rich* and *How to Start Your Own Business on a Shoestring and Earn Up to $100,000 per Year* are available from Parker Publishing Company Inc., West Nyack, N.Y. 10994.

papers. Soon you have 300 local young ladies taking ballet lessons in your school. Each student pays you $10 per week. Thus, your gross income is $3,000 per week.

Synergy Goes to Work for You

After a few months you decide that you want to expand. You consider selling ballet dance togs—the thin black tights the dancer wears while practicing. But you give up this idea when you find that the profit potential is too small. Why? Because you're just acting as a retailer and the profit per sale is only pennies. Further, your sales would be restricted to your students.

Looking around, you find a local indoor swimming pool, complete with its own building, land, diving boards, ladies' locker room, men's locker room, snack bar, ping pong tables, water treatment tanks, pumps, and recreation room, up for sale. Since you're already in a physical-culture type business—the ballet school—the swimming pool appeals to you. But you recognize that:

Any business that requires a large amount of equipment for its operation is a risky undertaking for a BWB.

So instead of buying the pool, you *rent* it for one year from the owner. In the lease you have an option to buy the pool or renew your lease for the next three years. If you buy the pool, the money you paid in rent will apply towards the purchase price.

You take over the pool and immediately:

* Offer reduced-price swimming lessons to your ballet students
* Form swimming clubs among local high school and college students
* Hold swimming meets for children and adults
* Invite local ladies' bridge clubs to swim for fun and health in the afternoon
* Hold Saturday night swim parties

Your business booms. Why? Synergy is at work. How? Like this:

* Your ballet school students come to your pool, enjoy themselves, tell their friends.
* The friends swim and enjoy it; they come back with other friends.
* Some of the friends, and friends of friends, decide to take your ballet lessons.

- Kids, and parents, come together, have fun, tell other kids and other parents.
- Your Ladies' Day afternoon swims are popular with the young and not-so-young mothers in the area. They hear of your ballet school and send their young daughters to it.
- Saturday night family swim parties bring you a good income and more word-of-mouth advertising.

The synergistic effect of the ballet school and swimming pool give you a gross income of $300,000 per year. After renting the pool a year you decide you know enough about the business to buy the pool. You do, using the $17,000 left over from the $20,000 state loan as your down payment. OPM and synergy are about to make you a millionaire.

Serendipity Helps You Find Your Fortune

Serendipity is the practical use of the well-known proverb "Seek and thou shalt find." Why? Because whenever you seek anything in life—such as wealth, position, reputation, etc.—you improve your chances for success. Often you'll find what you want, plus other benefits you didn't expect.

Serendipity is the unexpected finding of one benefit while looking for another.

In our first example, above, where you were looking for business real estate, you found speculative real estate as well. Serendipity helped you find the speculative real estate.

And in the second example, serendipity found you the indoor swimming pool. The pool is an excellent partner for your ballet school, and vice versa.

To put serendipity to work, just apply this one simple rule:

Look for the good things in life—in yourself, in others, and in business. Serendipity will see to it that you find more good than you seek!

You've now seen leverage, synergy, and serendipity at work in the area of local and state loans. Further, you've learned how and where to obtain local and state loans. So don't waste time. Get going—right now—on obtaining local or state aid for your business.

9

Bring Uncle Sam into Your Business

In my business travels throughout the world I meet thousands of foreign businessmen who say: "You American businessmen are the luckiest people in the world. Your government encourages business by offering you loans and various tax advantages. We don't have any of these advantages in our country."

Count Your Business Blessings

Yet when I travel to various parts of the United States I hear businessmen complaining about taxes, laws, rules, etc. Often I'll take one of these complainers aside and tell him:

You live in the greatest business country in the world. The most powerful government that ever existed since the beginning of time is ready to help you. So stop complaining, and start counting your business blessings!

Truly, as a citizen businessman, you have more wealth at your command than you ever dreamt possible. In this chapter I'll show you how to latch onto some of the billions of dollars Uncle Sam has ready for you. And by the time you finish this chapter I hope you're convinced that the United States is the greatest country ever—because it really is!

Know Your Loan Sources

There are at least a dozen federal agencies that make low-cost, long-term loans to small businesses in the United States. 'But, just what is a small business?" you ask. The Small Business Administration (SBA) defines a small business as a business which has:

- Gross sales of less than $1 million a year in retail or service activities
- Gross sales of less than $5 million a year in a wholesale business
- Less than 250 employees in a manufacturing business

If your firm is close to any of these limits, check with the SBA. You may find that the definitions have been changed recently or that you qualify under a special clause.

What Kinds of Loans Can You Obtain?

The SBA makes numerous different types of loans including loans for:

> Working capital
> Business equipment
> Real estate for business
> Repairs caused by natural disasters
> Debt retirement

The SBA lends more money to small firms than any other agency of the federal government. Also, the SBA has more money available for small businesses than any other agency. Since you can easily make some of this money yours, you should learn everything you can about the SBA. This chapter will give you much of the information you need. But to be certain you don't overlook any opportunities, be sure to contact your local SBA office. You'll find it listed in your phone book under U. S. Government.

Learn SBA Loan Amounts and Rates

Knowledge is power. When you know how much the SBA can lend, and at what rates, you're ready to do some comparison shopping. Let's get the facts you need down on paper here and now.

The amount of money you can borrow from the SBA can be as little as $1,000 or as much as $350,000. Probably the most common loan SBA makes to small businesses is $15,000. Why? Because this seems to be an amount sufficient for the needs of most small business firms.

Does this mean you have to be satisfied with $15,000, even though you need much more? No! You can borrow any amount you need, up to $500,000.

And—good news—your SBA loan will be at a lower interest rate than any other loan you might obtain from a bank, a finance company, or a private business source. Why will your SBA business loan be at such a low rate? Because our federal government wants to encourage small businesses to grow and expand. And providing capital is probably one of the best ways of achieving this important goal.

Further, your payoff period for an SBA business loan will be longer—usually six years—than any other source would allow you. This means your monthly loan payments will be lower, allowing you more money for yourself. And with the low interest rate charged, the total amount of interest you pay may be lower than with a short-term high-interest loan.

To summarize, your SBA business loan might be:

- Larger than a loan from another source
- At a lower interest rate
- Made for a longer period of time

So keep one key fact in mind at all times:

Your cheapest source of business financing is probably an SBA business loan. Such a loan can give you more money, faster.

Now let's look at the other side of the picture—namely the reasons why SBA rejects loan applications.

Why Does SBA Reject Loans?

The SBA has specific and definite reasons for rejecting loan applications. What I want to do in this section of the book is to list those reasons so you can avoid them.

The SBA, in general, won't make business loans

- To professional gamblers
- To businesses obtaining more than half their net sales from alcoholic beverages
- To newspapers, magazines, radio, or TV broadcasters
- For recreational facilities unless the general public benefits
- To lending or investment firms
- For speculative real estate
- For monopolistic businesses
- To businesses that can obtain funds from other sources

To obtain a fuller picture of these rules, contact your nearest SBA office. Just be sure your loan isn't refused for any of these reasons!

Other Sources of Federal Funds

Many other federal government agencies, departments, and administrations lend money to businesses. You should check out each of these loan sources if you think they can help you.

Federal loan sources worth checking out include:

> Agency for International Development
> Community Facilities Administration
> Export-Import Bank
> Federal Housing Administration
> Federal Reserve System
> Health, Education, and Welfare Agency
> Maritime Administration
> Office of Trade Adjustment
> Public Housing Administration
> Treasury Department of the U. S.
> Urban Renewal Administration

Each of these loan sources is located in Washington, D.C. To obtain details about the loan amount, interest rate, and payoff period, simply write the agency of your choice at Washington, D.C.

How to Be Sure Your Loan Is Approved

There are five words you must know to ensure that you obtain your business loan from the federal government. These words are:

- Records
- Write-up
- Application
- Reasons
- Future

Let's take a look at each of these words to see how you can put them to use when applying for your business loan. I want you to *get* that loan, without fail.

Records. If you're already in business, prepare a neat, accurate set of records showing your income and expenses. You should also prepare a profit and loss (P&L) statement showing how much profit your business has earned, or how much money it has lost. Here's a recommended arrangement for your P&L statement (Figure 9-1). This arrangement shows the cash flow for each month of the year.

MONTHLY PROFIT AND LOSS

Net sales		$———
Less: Material used	$———	
Direct labor	———	
Other manufacturing costs	———	
Cost of goods sold	$———	$———
Gross profit		
Less: Sales expense	$———	
General and administrative costs	———	
Operating profit	$———	$———

CASH FLOW

Cash balance (beginning of month)		$———
Receipts from receivables		———
Total available cash		———
Less disbursements:		
Trade payables	$———	
Direct labor	———	
Other manufacturing costs	———	
Sales expense	———	
General and administrative costs	———	
Fixed-asset additions	———	
Bank loans to be repaid	———	
Total disbursements		$———
Indicated cash shortage		———
Bank loans to be obtained		———
Cash balance (end of month)		$———
Materials purchased		$———

MONTH-END POSITION

Accounts receivable	$———
Inventory	———
Accounts payable	———
Bank loans payable	———

Figure 9-1

If you prepare, and use, a P&L statement like this, your chances of obtaining the loan you need are much better than if you have untidy, inaccurate records. So please, take my advice and prepare the neatest set of records you possibly can.

Write-up. Is your business brand new? Are you still in the planning stage for a business you have not yet opened? If you answer yes to either question, then you need a write-up for your business. And what is a write-up? It's a brief description of the:

- Business you plan
- Customers you'll serve
- Products you'll sell
- Services you'll offer
- Gross business volume expected
- Anticipated profits
- Future growth prospects

Your write-up will help you understand your business better. Further, you can give a copy of the write-up to each of the agencies to whom you apply for a loan. A well-prepared write-up can mean the difference between acceptance and rejection of your loan application. Further, you'll be better prepared to discuss your business with anyone, once you finish the write-up.

Application. Fill out the *proper* application for your loan. Though this may seem obvious, many BWBs overlook this important step in obtaining their loan. They either

- Don't fill out any application
- Fill out the wrong application
  or
- Give incomplete information

To avoid delays, wasted time, short tempers, and other problems, fill out the proper application neatly and completely. You'll be glad you did because your loan application will get faster attention and approval

Reasons. Have good *business* reasons for requesting a federal government loan. Earlier chapters list a number of acceptable, valid reasons for borrowing money for business purposes.

For surer and faster acceptance of a federal loan application, try to include in your reasons for requesting the loan:

- Data on how the community will benefit
- Number of jobs the loan will provide
- Average earnings of your workers

- Educational benefits to your workers
- Benefits to the U. S., if there are any

Federal loan officials lend taxpayers' money. Being dedicated employees, they want the money to do the most good. So be sure to include in your *business* reasons any advantages the community or your employees will gain from the loan. Then your chances for acceptance will be much greater.

Future. Try to include in your loan application, and in your write-up, the future prospects for your business. Federal loan officers are human —they want as much assurance as they can obtain that your business will grow and prosper. By including a sentence or two on the future of your business you may clinch the approval of your loan. So why leave it out?

Reach for the Big Money

Tom K. was a poor man when he reached his fiftieth birthday—the half-century mark. Yet Tom hadn't lost his drive to become rich. He still wanted to rake in the big money in his own business. But Tom recognized that he had to get rich *fast*, if he was to enjoy his money while he still had his health and vitality.

What could he do? He had no capital to speak of; his credit rating, while good, was not spectacular. There was only one answer. He'd have to hit the big money using OPM—other people's money.

Tom analyzed his situation and decided he needed a business that:

(1) Required essentially no inventory other than a few pencils and pieces of paper

(2) Would give him an immediate cash income

(3) Could be built up quickly

(4) Would bill customers in large amounts instead of small amounts

(5) Would use his skill, time, and energy in place of a large investment of capital

These business features are the same ones that any BWB—such as you or your friends—should seek when trying to start a business with little or no capital. Tom, at age 50, had spent enough time thinking about a business to isolate these features as important ones to a BWB.

Next, Tom analyzed himself to see how he could match his skills to the business features he set up. This think session with a pencil and piece of paper soon showed Tom that he:

- Had no capital
- Needed money quickly
- Possessed only one skill
- Must get working immediately

Accentuate Your Skills

The only positive item Tom could see in the above list was the fact that he had one skill. That skill? Foreign trade—import-export and related matters. Tom had studied foreign trade while he was in military service. From the time he was released until the present, Tom enjoyed predicting what the future foreign trade of various countries would be. Since this was his only skill, Tom decided that he had to find some way to market it at a profit.

Tom went to the public library in his town and began to research the business aspects of foreign trade. During this research he learned two negative and one positive fact about the money aspects of foreign trade. These facts were:

Negative: Government-employed foreign trade experts usually earn less than $10,000 per year.

Negative: Foreign trade experts employed by large corporations usually earn less than $15,000 per year.

Positive: Private foreign-trade consultants often receive as much as $50,000 per year from one client; and a good consultant can have many clients!

"I'll accentuate my skills," Tom said, "and go into the foreign trade business as a consultant."

Luckily, Tom soon found, a consulting business:

- Requires no inventory
- Gives an immediate cash income
- Can grow quickly

> • Can charge large fees
> • Operates mainly on the owner's skill

Thus, Tom's chosen business exactly met the features he earlier decided he wanted in a business. (Had the business been deficient in one or more features, Tom would have tried to alter the business until it met his requirements. Or he would "trade-off"; i.e., give up one desirable feature to gain another, more attractive, advantage.)

Bring Uncle Sam into Your Business

Tom decided he needed at least $5,000 in capital to start his business. He applied for loans at several banks and was turned down by each. That's when he decided to apply to the United States Government.

Taking a short write-up of his business with him, Tom applied to the federal government for a loan. His application was quickly approved and in a few weeks Tom received his loan check.

During his research Tom came across a book titled *Worldwide Riches Opportunities* published by IWS, P.O. Box 186, Merrick, N.Y. 11566, for $25. Issued annually, and updated regularly during the year, the book contains items on

* Foreign firms seeking U. S. products
* Manufacturing licenses sought by overseas firms
* Products offered for import to the U. S.
* Overseas sales representatives available

With more than 2,000 items such as those listed above available in each annual issue, Tom figured he could earn big fees:

* Finding U. S. products wanted by overseas firms
* Negotiating license agreements
* Contacting U. S. firms about imports available
* Checking out and appointing sales reps

Great Success Can Be Yours

Tom started business by contacting U. S. firms he thought could supply products wanted by overseas companies, as listed in the book *Worldwide Riches Opportunities*. He soon found that many U. S. firms were extremely interested in doing business overseas. So for each successful arrangement he negotiated between a U. S. firm and an overseas firm, Tom charged the U. S. firm $500. During his first month in business,

Tom negotiated ten arrangements, giving him a gross income of $5,000. This was exactly the amount Tom had borrowed to finance his business!

Another service Tom soon introduced was a listing, for his overseas clients, of U. S. firms engaged in a specific business or other activity. Tom compiled this list using data from the above book and a variety of other sources. He sells the list to overseas firms who need information about U. S. companies.

Within six months Tom built his business to a level where his gross income was more than $10,000 per month. Yet he:

- Carries no inventory
- Receives quick payment
- Invested no capital
- Is growing rapidly
- Sells his knowledge

If you're in Tom's situation, consider doing what he did. With some modest financial help you can quickly get started on building your fortune. (And, incidentally, there's still plenty of room in the foreign-trade business.)

Analyze Low-Capital Activities

Many people shy away from low-capital activities because they're afraid of failing. These people give all kinds of excuses for their fear, like:

- I don't have any experience
- My appearance isn't good enough
- People frighten me
- It may not work out

I love to meet someone who comes up with excuses like these. Why? Because I get genuine pleasure showing these people how wrong they are. Within just a few minutes I can convert them from the world's greatest pessimists to enthusiastic doers. And in a few months, by following my advice, they can be earning a big income. Many of these former pessimists write to say:

Becoming an optimist changed my life. It makes me feel better, earn more, and accomplish greater things in life.

Most of these letters conclude with: "It's true; everything you said is true! I didn't believe it when you told me but I do believe it now."

You Can Get Good Advice

Why people won't believe one another I don't know. Perhaps it's because many people believe everyone in this world is out to "get" them in
one way or another. When they meet someone who is really trying to
help them—with no strings attached—they don't know how to react to
such a novel situation.

The key idea to keep in mind while reading any of my books on
earning money is this:

> You have a friend who's willing to help you—if you're ready to
> listen and learn.

You *can* make money with only a small investment of capital—which
you can borrow from someone else. But the amount you can earn with
only a small investment of capital is, of course, restricted. "I knew there
was a catch in your method," you laugh.

Yes, there is a restriction on your earnings potential. Much research
in my own activities, and the careers of many of my outstandingly successful friends, shows:

> With only a small capital investment ($5,000 to $15,000) and work-
> ing with just one secretary, you can easily earn between $150,000
> and $300,000 per year. To earn more than this you usually must make
> a larger investment.

Let's take a look at these income figures. If you earn $300,000 a year
in your own business you'll be a millionaire in a little more than three
years. With earnings of $150,000 per year, it will take you just under
seven years to reach the millionaires' level.

Either way, friend, if you reach your money goal, I'll feel that I've
been of some help to you. Why? Well truly, you can't become a millionaire in *any* business in much less than three years! So if you want to
say there's a catch in the method, there is—three years. But so is there
a catch in every other method—three years!

Stay Out of Business Trouble

I've watched thousands of businessmen and women struggle to earn a
living in their own business. Some hit it big—they become millionaires.
Others struggle for years, trying to achieve their dream. Why do some
people achieve their goal quickly while others miss it or take much

longer to reach their objective? I don't have all the answers but I believe I have most of the important ones. Probably the key answer for *you* is this:

Most people fail to reach the big money because they refuse to think and plan their future BEFORE they take action.

When people fail to plan ahead, they lose control of the future. So you see them reacting to external situations, instead of acting the way they really want to. Remember this:

When we think and plan ahead, WE control the future—the future doesn't control us!

So instead of being a yo-yo on the end of a string, you are the captain in command of your ship. Winds and waves may cause you to slow down, speed up, or alter course. But you are still in command—you control *your* future. And that's the way it should be in business—*you* should be in command at all times.

You can stay out of business trouble by planning ahead. How? By steering clear of trouble-making business situations. Here are a number of such business situations which may cause problems. Whenever you meet these conditions in a prospective business, be careful.

- Large product inventory is required
- Legal problems are numerous
- Orders are for small amounts
- Extensive credit is required
- Payroll is large
- Only union labor can be used
- Special, expensive machines are needed
- Product or process is extremely fragile, sensitive
- Business requires a skill you don't have
- Excessive capital needed for business

Of course, there are other conditions that can lead to trouble in your business. But the above ten items are ones about which you should be particularly alert. Don't reject a business because it has one or more of these characteristics—just be extremely cautious about it.

Have Faith in Uncle Sam

My business interests take me all over the world. In one of my activities I lecture to top engineers and scientists in key industries throughout the world. Each year, when I return to the United States after one of my lecture tours, I marvel at the industrial greatness of America. And how can we explain this superiority of American industry?

The U. S. Government, through its many loans to industry, its tax laws, and other industry-oriented plans, is one of the greatest encouragers of business and personal growth in the world. Most people complain bitterly about income taxes and similar government laws. Yet if you study our tax laws carefully you will soon see that they are directed at encouraging business growth. How? By offering:

- Liberal depreciation credits
- Business expense deductions
- Advertising expense deductions
- Rent, light, and heat deductions

Stated briefly, there is no legitimate business expense which can't be deducted This means you can deduct expenses for current business items, as well as for future business items. Thus, you are allowed to spend, tax-free, as much as you need to ensure the healthy growth of your business. Such spending can make you a millionaire within a few years while permitting you to live a much richer personal life.

It's for these reasons that you seldom hear businessmen complain for long about income taxes. In fact, I have a theory that says:

The vitality of American business stems, in large measure, from the ingenuity businessmen develop while learning how to earn a profit under our tax system.

Just as a man who's married to a sharp-tongued woman learns to be adroit with his responses, so too does a businessman become a better profit builder as he learns to live with our tax system. In fact, I often recommend that BWBs study the Schedule C and corporate tax forms before going into business. These forms and their accompanying instructions are available free from your local Internal Revenue Service office. During your study of the forms and instructions you'll learn a great deal about business and business taxes.

Many BWBs, after studying these forms, say: "Gee, I never realized how many legitimate deductions I could take. Show me how to get started in my own business. I want to make as much money as I can, as soon as I can!" Yes, friend, our tax laws really are liberal when compared with the tax laws of other nations.

Don't Be Ashamed to Use Government Money

Many BWBs think of a government loan as similar to being on the dole. This is ridiculous. As a citizen or resident of the United States you are entitled to help from your federal government. Remember:

The government WANTS to help you earn a fortune in your own business. So use the help that's offered to you.

The BWB who has drive power never turns away from a government loan. Instead, he asks: "Where's the nearest loan office? What hours is it open? How long will I have to wait for my money?" There's no thought of the dole in this person's mind.

So count your blessings instead of hiding in the trap of outmoded beliefs. The government money with which you can build your fortune is there waiting for you. Go and get it—now!

10

Sell Stocks and Bonds to Raise Capital

All the ways of obtaining capital we've discussed thus far involve *borrowing* money. And when you borrow money you *must* repay—usually according to some fixed payment schedule. Thus, borrowing has one major disadvantage; i.e.,

> When you borrow money for business purposes you are taking on a fixed payment obligation. Such an obligation can overburden you at a time when your income is low.

Once a BWB realizes this fact of business life he quickly asks, "Is there any way I can obtain capital for my business without having a fixed repayment obligation?"

My answer is yes, there is. You can sell stock in your company, *provided your company is organized as a corporation.*

"Great!" you say. "Tell me more, as quickly as possible."

I will, but I want you to read this chapter very, very carefully. Why? Because it may contain the key to great wealth for you. So let's get started.

Know the Details of Stock Sales

You can organize a corporation in any state or almost any country to conduct nearly every kind of business. Certain businesses—such as the practice of medicine, dentistry, engineering, and some other professions—cannot be incorporated in many states. But these do not concern us here because we're thinking of businesses that might interest you, such as:

Mail order
Real estate
Retail sales
Auto repair
Import-export
Business services

Any of these, and any of the usual businesses you might see on Main Street, U. S. A., can be incorporated. And if your business is incorporated you can sell stock to the public. But *your business must be incorporated before you can sell stock to the public.*

Advantages of Going Public

When you sell stock in your firm to the public, your lawyers and accountants say you *have gone public.* What they mean is that part of your company is owned by the public—the people who bought stock in your firm.

When you go public you:

(1) Obtain needed business funds
(2) Do not have fixed repayments to make
(3) Need never repay the money you receive
(4) Pay dividends only when justified by your company's earnings
(5) Can obtain millions of dollars for business purposes
(6) Don't have to give up control of your business

Thus, going public can put money in your company's bank account quickly and with little effort on your part. You can issue stock for any legitimate business purposes, such as:

- Financing new buildings or equipment
- Meeting current bills
- Paying off loans or notes
- Conducting an advertising campaign
- Buying out other companies

There is hardly any limit to the business reasons for which you can sell stock to the public. What's more, you can issue stock as often as you need money. Most firms, however, sell enough stock to satisfy their current and projected money needs and then stay out of the money market for a year or so. With an attractive record of income growth, you can go back to the public again and again for more and more money. The largest firms in the world do it—why shouldn't you?

Ten Key Questions on Selling Stock

If you're a typical beginning wealth builder (BWB), you're probably full of questions at this very moment. Since I believe I know most of your questions, I'll try to answer them right now.

Q. My business is brand new. I haven't yet made one sale. Can I still sell stock in my company?

A. Yes! You need not even have an office for the company. You can still sell stock in your company if (*a*) your firm is incorporated, (*b*) enough shares of stock have been authorized, and (*c*) you have a mailing address (your home address can be used if you don't yet have a business address).

Q. How much will it cost me to incorporate my business?

A. The cost of incorporating your business varies from state to state and country to country. Probably the smallest amount you will spend on incorporating is about $50.

This money is for:

- State registration fee
- Notary fee
- State tax on stock
- Postage
- Corporate forms and seal

You may have a few other, or different, charges in your state, but the fees usually are similar from one state to another. If you hire a lawyer to incorporate your business he will charge you a total of at least $100, and possibly much more. The legal fees you are charged depend, to some extent, on your ability to pay; i.e., how much money you have.

Q. Should I hire a lawyer to incorporate my business for me?

A. Yes, if you plan to go public. In fact, it's wise to hire a lawyer for every incorporation. *But a lawyer is not necessary in every state.* In many states you can incorporate the business yourself simply by filling out the necessary forms and paying the required fees.

Q. Should I incorporate my business in Delaware, as many large companies do?

A. Yes, if you reside in, and operate your business in, Delaware. But if you reside in another state and operate your business in your home state, you will probably be better off incorporating in your home state. Why? Because of a valuable provision in the law which allows you to make an *intrastate* (only in your own state) stock offering *without* registering the offering with the Securities and Exchange Commission (SEC). This provision can save you heaps of money and time. We'll be talking more about it later in this chapter.

Q. Isn't it expensive to sell stock?

A. No! You can use a typewritten, mimeographed or offset-printed offering circular (description of your company and its business). While some firms spend $7,000 or more to have their offering circular printed, you should be able to get by for less than $100, if you follow the hints we give you later.

Q. I don't have a dime. How can I afford to go public?

A. *Borrow* the money you need. Repay your lenders using corporate cash obtained from your stock offering. This is completely legal, valid, and practical. What's more, companies do it every day of the week. In using this technique, you lend the company money which you borrow. Then the company repays you when it has the cash.

Q. Can I get into trouble selling stock in my company?

A. There's very little chance of running into trouble when you sell stock to the public if: (a) you are completely honest in all statements you publish or make about your company, (b) you reveal all pertinent facts about your company, and (c) you do not use inside information about the company to earn personal profits. While there are periodic headlines about company officials being sued by stockholders or being tried by a government agency for violation of securities regulations, you needn't worry. Why? Because these cases usually relate to:

- Large corporations
- Enormous sums of money
- Disenchanted stockholders
- Firms in the public eye

As an official of a small, hard-working, honest corporation you have nothing to fear.

Q. Can I do all the paper work needed for a stock offering?

A. Yes. In some states very little paper work is needed. In other states you'll have more work to do. The best way to find out what paper work must be done is to check with your local securities board or agency.

Q. For how long can I sell stock in my company?

A. For as long as you have shares available. Most firms, however, try to sell the shares they have available as quickly as possible—in about 90 days, or less. If your stock is a "hot issue"; i.e., your business is one which the public thinks is booming—you might be able to sell out all your shares in a few hours. The important points to keep in mind are:

- You can sell stock for years
- Money received for stock is tax-free
- Several classes of stock can be used
- Warrants can also be used

Q. How can I make my stock more attractive to the public?

A. There are several ways to make your stock more attractive to the public. These are:

(1) Be in a hot-issue business
(2) Offer several grades of stock
(3) Include warrants

"How," you ask, "can I tell which are the hot issues?"

That's easy. Just read the financial pages of any large city newspaper. You'll quickly see which businesses have hot issues. Typical hot new issues in recent years included firms in the fields of:

- Electronics
- Computers
- Nursing homes
- Publishing
- Medical equipment
- Oceanography
- Business office equipment

When you write your prospectus, try to mention in the prospectus one or more of the hot-issue activities if your firm is, or might be, doing business in any of the hot-issue areas. But keep one point clearly in mind. This is:

A prospectus must be clear, accurate, and to the point. Any exaggerations which mislead investors can be troublesome.

Another way to increase the public interest in your stock issue is to offer several grades of stock, such as:

- Regular common stock
- Convertible stock
- Common stock with warrants

Regular common stock is what we've been discussing throughout this chapter. You'll receive more details about this grade of stock as we go along.

Convertible stock and bonds offer the buyer an incentive. Why? Because, after a certain period of time, he can convert his holdings into a larger number of shares of common stock. Hopefully, the common-stock shares will be worth more at a future date than they are today. Thus, the buyer of your stock buys today in the hope of future growth tomorrow.

Warrants also offer the buyer an incentive. Here's how the warrants work. Each share of stock you sell has a warrant attached to it. This warrant allows the buyer of a common share to purchase one or more common shares of the stock at a future date for a stated price. Hopefully, the future price of the stock will be higher than the price offered to warrant holders. If this happy condition occurs, and it usually does in new growth firms, the buyer makes a handsome profit. For instance:

Stock price at first public sale:	$10 per share
Warrant stock price, three years hence:	$7 per share
Actual stock price, three years hence:	$35 per share
Profit per share on warrant:	$28 per share
Profit per share of common stock:	$25 per share
Total profit per share and warrant:	$53 per share

Thus, the buyer of a share of your stock and its attached warrant could increase his holdings by $53/$10 = 5.3 times. This is the magic grow power of OPM and an expanding business.

How to Sell Your Stock

As an officer of your firm,

- President
- Executive vice-president
- Vice-president
- Secretary

or other elected officer, you are allowed, in many states, to sell your stock yourself. "So what's that to me?" you ask. Just this:

As an officer of your corporation you can sell stock to the public. This eliminates the need of a stockbroker and saves his commission.

Most new, small firms aren't too interesting as stock offerings to stockbrokers because these firms are, in their early years:

- Usually unknown
- Highly risky
- Relatively unprofitable

So the right to sell shares in your company is a valuable grant to you. While you may dislike selling, take some advice from me and remember this:

When you have a piece of the action; i.e., you own part of a company, your leverage and profit potential are enormous.

Be a Big-Time Winner

I earn money in many different ways. Further, I've earned big money in more ways than I can remember. Here's a brief listing of current ways I earn money:

1. Mail-order sales
2. Corporate dividends
3. Book royalties
4. Retail sales
5. Management consulting
6. Seminar lectures
7. Article publication
8. Foreign translations
9. Technical editing
10. Brochure publishing
11. Salaried executive
12. Sales commissions
13. Private tutoring
14. Business consulting
15. Company ownership
16. Profit sharing
17. Manuscript typing
18. Stock market
19. Marine-product sales
20. Book publishing

Each of these activities currently pays me a significant income. Yet if I had to give up every source of income except one, the source that I'd hang onto would be company ownership. Why? Because:

As owner of a company you have many potential sources of income from all over the world. And, with hard work, you can increase the size of your company to as large as you want. You can really win BIG.

Every other source of income—a salary, book royalties, consulting, lecturing, etc.—has certain built-in limitations. True, you can earn $50,000 to $100,000, or more, per year at these activities. But your income doesn't grow the way it does when you have a piece of the action in a go-go swinging company.

Ted C. owns shares of stock in his own company. Recently Ted watched the value of these shares, which are traded in the over-the-counter market, rise from 40¢ a share to $2.00 per share in two months. This means that Ted's 100,000 shares rose from a value of $40,000 to $200,000 in two months! Show me any other business or profession that can give you growth like that.

From the leverage standpoint, that is:

Using a small amount of cash to control a large amount of OPM, having a piece of your own company can't be beat.

Ted C. invested about $200 to start his own company. Not only did he see its business and income grow—he also watched with delight as the value of his shares skyrocketed.

Make Yourself a Millionaire

I travel throughout the United States, Europe, and many other countries, taking care of my many business interests. During these trips I talk to hundreds of business people in large cities, small towns, and in agricultural areas. Yet all these business people—be they men or women in a city or town, or on a farm—have one general, universal goal. They want to *make a million*, be their million measured in dollars, marks, francs, pounds, etc. Remember:

People's wants are basically the same everywhere. Geography has little influence on changing these wants.

Regardless of where you live, or where the people you meet live, most of us want:

- An attractive home or apartment
- A car of our choice
- A hobby we enjoy
- High-class vacations
- Well-fitting clothes
- A good education for our kids
- Some extra cash for that rainy day

Most of the world agrees with Oscar Wilde, who said, "When I was young I *thought* that money was the most important thing in life; now that I am old, I *know* it is."

You can, with a positive outlook, and by *using* the hints given in this book, make yourself a millionaire. Others have done exactly that; so can you.

Make Reg A Work for You

Manny K. wanted to own a string of bakeries. Don't ask me why any man would want to become a big-time baker—Manny just did.

He came to me for advice. On analyzing his money needs we found he had to raise at least $1 million. Manny, we discovered, could go public to raise this money. But the amount involved would require a major underwriting effort. And Manny and his company, in my opinion, weren't ready for that yet. His business ideas were too new; he didn't have enough experience, capital, or willing backers. So I suggested: "Manny, go the Reg A route."

"How?" he asked.

"Form four small companies. Have each company make a Reg A or $300,000 stock offering. This will bring you four times $300,000 or $1.2 million."

Manny snapped his fingers in glee. "Darn it; why didn't I think of that," he said excitedly.

"I'm not finished yet," I said. "After you make your four public offerings you'll have $200,000 more than you need. And if you ever get tired of being president of four companies, all you need do is merge the four into one."

That's exactly what Manny did. Today he's the happy owner of a string of bakeries that keep him in a very comfortable style—so comfortable that he never need worry again. He can truly say that he made Reg A work for him. So can you, if you plan properly.

Four Steps to Using Reg A

Regulation A is an *exemption* from registering your stock with the SEC. The SEC defines your issue as "small" if the *gross* proceeds from your stock sales do not exceed $300,000 in any 12-month period. To use Reg A for your company:

(1) Call or write your local SEC office and request a free copy of "Regulation A General Exemption from Registration Under the Securities Act of 1933." This useful publication gives you what you need to know, plus many useful forms.

(2) Prepare your offering prospectus. Take my advice—write the prospectus yourself. Don't pay someone to do it—you can do a better job than he can. If you've never seen a prospectus for a small stock issue, call or visit a stock broker and ask him for copies of several recent ones. The publication mentioned above tells you what to include in your prospectus.

(3) File your notification on SEC Form 1-A with the SEC at least 10 days before the offering date—the date on which you plan to start selling stock.

(4) Start selling your stock, unless the SEC restrains you from doing so and requests more information about the company, its business, or its officers.

Try an Intrastate Offering

With an intrastate offering, i.e., an offering whose stock is sold only to the residents of the state in which the firm is incorporated, and in which it does *some* business, you need not file any papers with the SEC. Your exemption is automatic.

You may, however, have to file papers with your state. But the rules of most states are relatively simple. In fact, many states actively encourage firms within their boundaries to go public because this builds the state wealth and increases the tax revenues. For these reasons, most states have only the simplest registration requirements.

Some states have *no* registration requirements at all for stocks sold to the public. Which states, you ask? I have a list on my desk as I write, but I hesitate to include it here because:

State laws change frequently. So before making any public offering of the securities of your company, check the regulations in your state.

Watch for Intrastate Traps

Just as state highway police set speed traps for those who endanger their own lives and the lives of others by speeding, so too are there traps in intrastate securities offerings. And since I want you to be as successful as possible, in the quickest way possible, you should be aware of these traps. Then, hopefully, you'll be able to avoid them.

The items you should watch out for are:

- Resales to out-of-state residents
- Offering circular

Resales to non-residents: You *lose* your exemption from SEC registration requirement, or notification requirement, whichever applies, if you sell as little as *one share* to a non-resident of the state in which you are making the offering. Or you can lose the exemption if a resident re-sells the stock he purchased to a non-resident *during* the time you are offering stock to the public.

This is a critically important point that you'll want to keep in mind at all times. The buyers of your stock can re-sell it to whomever they please *after* the offering ends—usually 90 to 180 days after you begin the offering.

When large numbers of shares are being re-sold, ask the seller to delay, if possible, his re-sale for as long as possible after the end of your offering. Then there's no chance of anyone inferring that the original purchase was not for investment but for re-sale, thereby causing you to lose your exemption.

Offering circular: Be certain that your offering circular, or prospectus (both terms are used for the same document), clearly specifies on its front cover: *These securities are offered for sale only to the residents of the State of ————, and may not be offered for resale outside the State until 90 days after the close of this offering.* With such a warning on your offering circular, there is hardly any danger of your being accused of planning a quick resale of your stock outside the state.

To summarize, when making an intrastate offering:

- Sell *only* to state residents
- Do not allow out-of-state resales during the offering
- Delay big resales until after the offering closes
- Write your offering circular carefully

Build Instant Wealth for Yourself

Many BWBs thinking about selling stock in their company concentrate on the money that will flow into the company treasury—say $100,000, $300,000, or even $1,000,000. This they call *instant wealth*. And, in a way, it is. Why? Because you retain 51 percent of the shares offered for sale. This gives you control of the company, and its funds.

There's another source of wealth available to you when you go public. And this source can be of much greater importance to you than the money received from the initial offering.

What is this other source of wealth for you? It is the:

- Growth in value of *your* shares
- Buying power of your *company's* shares
- Borrowing power of *either* group of shares

To see how this works, let's put you in business for a few minutes.

Make a Million This Year

Let's say that you form a corporation to engage in a business that interests you. As part of the corporation charter you authorize an issue of one million shares of stock at no par value.

You, as founder of the corporation, take 350,000 shares of stock. For your public issue you reserve 300,000 shares which you plan to sell at $1.00 per share. The remaining 350,000 shares will be left in the company for possible future sale. To start this company you invested $500 of your personal funds.

You and the other officers of your firm, whom you appointed, sell 100,000 shares of stock to the public. Then a small brokerage firm hears of your stock and volunteers to sell the remaining 200,000 shares. You agree, and quickly receive $160,000 from the broker. His expenses, he reports, are about 20 percent, or 0.20 ($200,000) = $40,000. With the cash from the 100,000 shares you and your officers sold, the total received from the offering is $100,000 + $160,000 = $260,000.

Since a market has "been made" by your broker; i.e., shares have been sold to the public, a price is established for your stock.

As time passes your company prospers. You:

- Issue earnings statements
- Report new developments to local papers
- Start construction of a factory

Your broker keeps in close touch and reports to you the daily price of your stock on the over-the-counter market. You watch with pleasure as the *Bid Price*, the price people are willing to pay, rises from a $1.00 per share to $1.50, $2.00, $2.50.

One day, about eight months after your stock offering, your broker calls and says: "I have some great news for you. Yesterday the bid price hit $3.00 per share."

You whistle and slump in your office chair. Why? Because you own 350,000 shares of stock worth $3 per share. This means *you are worth* the product of the two, or $3 (350,000) = $1,050,000! In less than a year you've built a $500 investment into a $1 million fortune. And besides your stock profits you have $260,000 in the corporate kitty to spend as you wish on business items such as:

- Your salary
- Travel and entertainment
- Auto rental
- Expense-account charges
- Credit-card costs

What better way can you find to make your fortune on OPM?

Amazing Secrets of Successful Stock Offerings

In the company I set up for you in the above example, your stock share price tripled; i.e., it went from $1 to $3 in less than one year. I assumed that your stock tripled in value because I didn't want you to think I was exaggerating. Yet I personally know of the following *actual* cases of new-stock issue price increases:

- $1.75 offering price to $21.50 in 18 months
- $7.50 offering price to $30.00 in 1 week
- $1.00 offering price to $12.00 in 2 weeks
- $2.00 offering price to $16.00 in 10 days

With 350,000 shares of the first stock you would be worth $7,525,000 in 18 months! How did a stock grow that fast? The answer is simple. By using the amazing secrets of successful stock offerings. These secrets are:

- Use well-planned publicity for your company
- Publish profit results widely
- Play up new developments
- Get as much news as possible for inventions
- Publicize executive promotions

Thus, well-planned and properly timed publicity of all types can make your stock jump upwards in leaps that will thrill your bank account. And you don't have to be a public-relations expert to obtain publicity that pays off big. Simple, typewritten releases are gladly accepted by the newspapers and magazines.

For Great Wealth, Obey the Rules

Recent developments among federal and state securities agencies require that you, as an *insider* in your corporation, be:

- Sure all publicity is accurate, complete
- Certain that profits aren't made on inside info
- Careful not to mislead the public

Today the securities rules are so complex that you need an attorney to guide you, unless you're a stock expert yourself. For a complete monthly guide to the latest news about stock offerings and many other ways of quickly building wealth, I suggest you subscribe to *International Wealth Success*, mentioned previously.

Try Bond Sales Also

Bonds are different from stocks in that your corporation must repay the money received for the bond. The time period for a bond to mature

—be paid off—can be long—5, 10, 15, 20 years, or more. But the money must eventually be repaid to the purchaser of the bond. Also, you must, if you want to retain a good name for your corporation, pay interest each year on the bond.

To sell bonds you issue a prospectus similar to that you prepare for stocks. You must also obtain approval from federal and state authorities to sell your bonds. Since bonds are just another form of borrowing, I don't recommend that you sell bonds unless you can't borrow in any other way.

Become a Magic Fortune Builder

You *can* earn your fortune quickly and easily. I know because I've watched thousands of people do it. Further, I've done it several times myself. In this chapter I recommend that you build your fortune by going public. If I've motivated you, great. If I haven't motivated you to the point where you're ready to make a public stock offering, then I ask you to reconsider these facts:

- Any properly organized corporation can sell stock to the public
- You, personally, can sell the stock, if you enjoy selling
- If you don't enjoy sales work, hire an underwriter to sell your stock
- Keep in mind at all times that the money you receive from a public stock offering:
  - Doesn't have to be repaid
  - Is interest-free
  - Is tax-free
  - Can be used for any corporate purpose
  - Will pay *your* salary
  - Can repay corporate loans

Go public and watch your wealth grow far beyond your rosiest dreams. Remember—*Money is the touchstone that makes a wish a fact.* Turn your wishes into facts by going public today. Action builds fortunes; caution leads only to a mediocre income.

11

Ten Thousand Ready Sources
of Money

There's a well-known expression people use when they want action from someone who's done a certain amount of talking. You've heard the expression and can probably guess what it is, namely—"Put your money where your mouth is."

Well, I've done some talking and I'm now ready to show you where the money is. But before I do I want to alert you to several facts of life about borrowing money.

Be Professional in Your Business Life

Many beginning wealth builders (BWBs) fail to recognize one key point of business. This point is:

You must be professional in all your business dealings, if you are to be outstandingly successful.

Now what do I mean by being professional? Here's what I mean. You should:

- Have a *printed* business letterhead
- *Type* all business correspondence
- Maintain a *permanent* business address
- Have a business *telephone*

"But I can't afford these things," you say. "I'm just getting started." You *can* afford them if you save some money. A printed letterhead won't cost you more than $10 in small quantities. You can rent a portable typewriter for about $5 per month. Lastly, you can use your home address and home telephone as your business address and phone. If you don't want to use your home address, use a mail and phone service, or a post-office mail box. So you see, you really *can* get started for just a few dollars.

Accentuate the Positive

Use only your printed stationery when dealing with lenders—no matter how small the lender may be. Keep this key fact in mind:

The lender has what you want. Do everything possible to convince the lender that he'd be making a good business decision to lend you money. Be professional in your dealings!

An attractive letterhead goes a long way towards convincing any lender that you mean business. Be sure to type each letter you send him. Remember:

When you're just starting your wealth-building program, you don't have much to offer the lender. So accentuate the positive!

Use These Lender Lists

Following is a comprehensive list of publications in which you can find the names, addresses, and telephone numbers of thousands of lenders—banks, finance companies, brokerage houses, etc. These list are of two types: (a) free, and (b) moderate-price.

To get the most information from these lists of lenders, study the lists carefully. The one advantage of the moderate-price lists is that they classify more precisely than the free lists do the types of loans lenders are ready to make. Thus, if you're looking for 100 percent financing of real estate, you'll have to hunt through the free list by calling or writing each real-estate lender on the list. The lists you pay for classify the lenders so you can easily find a number of firms or organizations willing to lend 100 percent on real estate.

SOURCES OF LENDER NAMES AND ADDRESSES

Telephone Company Yellow Pages for New York City, Boston, Washington, D.C., Atlanta, Ga., Miami, Fla., Chicago, Ill., New Orleans, La., Dallas and Houston, Texas, Denver, Colo., San Francisco and Los Angeles, Calif. *The Yellow Pages* for these cities contain listings of more than 5,000 lenders. To find these lenders, look up the following entries:

> Banks
> Factors
> Financial Consultants
> Financing
> Loans (Business, Commercial, Industrial, Personal)
> Mortgages

Once you find a suitable number of lenders, call or write each lender. Never, never, write in longhand! Type your letter. If you write in longhand you're almost certain *not* to receive a reply.

If you don't have a telephone, go to a large local library. Many libraries have collections of *Yellow Pages* directories for cities all over the U.S. Thus, you can do your financial research free of charge in the comfort of your library. However, if you want personal copies of the directories of other cities, you can purchase them at nominal cost from the Telephone Company. Just call your local operator for details.

Business Capital Sources, $15, published by IWS Inc., P. O. Box 186, Merrick, N. Y. 11566. Lists hundreds of lenders interested in making a variety of loans—real-estate, inventory, business, personal, operating-fund, compensating balance, time-deposit, etc. Also gives much information about loans available from the Small Business Administration (SBA), and shows how to go public.

How to Raise Money to Make Money, by William J. Casey, $15, Institute for Business Planning, 2 W. 13 St., N.Y., N. Y. 10011. Contains numerous useful hints on how and when to borrow money for business purposes. Gives helpful pointers on preparing a financial statement for your business. Contains a few names of government organizations making business loans.

A Handbook of Small Business Finance, 50¢, Government Printing Office, Washington, D. C. 20402. Gives many useful pointers on borrowing money for your business, plus a list of a few government agencies willing to lend money for business purposes.

A Survey of Federal Government Publications of Interest to Small Business, 50¢, Government Printing Office, Washington, D. C. 20402. Lists a number of useful financial publications, some of which contain names of capital sources.

Worldwide Riches Opportunities, $25, IWS Inc., P. O. Box 186, Merrick, N. Y. 11566. Contains the names and addresses of more than 2,500

overseas firms that are often willing to lend money to firms with whom
they do business. Further, many of these firms will grant long-term credit
when you do business with them. This combination of cash and credit
can put you on easy street if you're interested in doing business with
overseas firms.

Now Go and Get Your Money

The above sources of the names of lenders are all you need to get on
the road to wealth using OPM. If you use the first two and the last
reference, you'll have the names of more than 10,000 lenders here and
abroad. With such a comprehensive list, it will be easy for you to obtain
the money you need. So start now to get your money—today. Using the
above references, your letterhead, and telephone, you can work in the
comfort and privacy of your own home and soon have the money you
want for your business.

12

Magic Techniques
of Loan Pyramiding

Many people think it is sinful to owe on more than one loan at one time. And a few people even think it is wrong to owe anything to anyone. Fortunately, the number of people holding either belief is rapidly declining, particularly in business.

Capital Is Business Fuel

Recognize, here and now, that capital (money) is the fuel that provides every business with its power. And in most businesses today the capital is OPM—other people's money. So why shouldn't you use OPM in your business?

Another little-known fact about modern business is this:

Most companies have more than one source of borrowed money, and many firms have more than one loan at one time.

"How can that be?" you ask. "I've always heard that you couldn't have more than one loan at a time."

"True, but this one-loan talk is for careless people who might overextend themselves if they knew they could take out more than one loan at a time. It doesn't apply to careful business people who put borrowed money to work to learn a profit."

During my world travels I talk to many business people. And almost all of them become envious when they talk about the possibilities of business loans in the United States. "If I had your loan sources I'd be a millionaire in three years," many of these business people say.

What Is Loan Pyramiding?

Loan pyramiding is a valuable technique which can make *you* a millionaire. While loan pyramiding is a valuable and powerful way of building fast riches, I don't recommend that everyone use this method. Why? Because loan pyramiding requires some previous *business* experience. If you don't have any business experience, wait until you have a year or two of experience in your own business. Then you'll be better equipped to handle any problems that may arise.

Just what is this technique and how does it work?

Loan pyramiding is the technique of using the money obtained from one loan to purchase or control assets which serve as the collateral for another loan while paying income to the borrower. Using this technique, as many as a dozen or more loans can be pyramided.

Loan Pyramiding Will Work for You

Let's take a closer look at a typical loan pyramid to see how it might work for you. While we are looking at the situation we'll imagine that you're interested in going into the motel business. And, incidentally, this is a good business to try to enter because the:

- Hours are short
- Profit is high
- People you meet are interesting
- Help need not be skilled
- Land can appreciate in value
- Future growth potential is excellent

You might say that any business related to the automobile anywhere in the world has a great potential. Why? Because the auto is always the "in" thing. For example, in the Washington, D.C. area, authorities estimate that the towns and cities spend $21,000 on highways, parking spaces, and other facilities for every new automobile that's put on the street. In what other business are the authorities so generous and cooperative?

How to Make Back-to-Back Deals

You see a motel advertised that interests you. We'll assume that you know something about the motel business—you've read a few books about it, as well as many of the trade magazines serving the field. Also, you've looked at a number of motels with the idea of purchasing one.

When you visit the motel you saw advertised, you're immediately struck with its rightness for you. The motel has everything you want:

- Good appearance
- Fine location
- Steady income
- Profitable rooms

You inquire about the price. The owner is asking $300,000 for the motel with a down payment of $10,000 cash. You have $5,000 you've saved from your salary on a job. Previous talks with bank officials in your town indicated that you could easily borrow $5,000 on a personal signature loan.

After some discussion with the seller, you manage to get him to reduce the price to $290,000 with $10,000 cash. You deposit $1,000 as a binder for the deal and go to the bank to borrow money. Since you've done some exploring for business capital in the past, you don't have any trouble obtaining the money. The bank credits your checking account with the $5,000 you borrowed.

You now have more than $9,000 in the bank. Drawing it out, you make the balance of the down payment on the motel.

Once you take over the motel, the business continues to be good—it even grows a little. You are pleased with the idea of controlling a $290,000 property with only $10,000 down.

Three months after taking over the motel another motel suddenly comes on the market at an excellent price because the aged owner passed away. The estate wants to sell the motel as quickly as possible. "This," you say to yourself "is my chance to put through back-to-back deals."

Building Your Pyramid Fast

You go back to the same bank that lent you the $5,000 to buy the first motel. It takes you only a few minutes to tell the loan officer that:

- Business is excellent
- Future prospects are great
- You "own" a big motel
- You're $300,000 richer than three months ago
- You need $20,000 cash for another motel

The loan officer is so impressed he takes you over and introduces you to the bank's junior vice-president. You tell your story quickly again and the junior vice-president is most favorably impressed. "We'd be delighted to make the loan," he says with a smile. "Mr. So-and-so," (the loan officer) "will handle the details. And the next time you're passing by, stop in to see me. If you have time, we'll have lunch together."

Ten minutes later you walk out of the bank with a $20,000 check in your pocket. Your head is spinning slightly, and you owe a lot more money than you did when you got out of bed that morning. But within a few days you will be the owner of another motel and your income will be zooming. Now let's analyze why you were able to get the second —and larger—loan so quickly.

Your second loan was approved because:

1. You're a person of substance; i.e., you control a large investment
2. You have proven yourself by taking on, and making payments on, such a large debt
3. Your future is bright—business is improving
4. You were frank with the bank—you told them what you owe

Though it may sound silly, the facts of business life are:

The more you owe, the greater your chances for success. The less you owe, the lower your chances are for hitting the big money.

With the $20,000 of OPM you take control of a motel valued at $500,000. Thus, you control $300,000 + $500,000 = $800,000 worth of property. You are fast on your way to controlling a million dollars worth of property.

Sing a Song of Wealth

Within a few months your reputation as a highly skillful motel operator has grown in your local area. You attend motel association meetings, make a few speeches before the right industry groups, and advise some investors who're thinking of putting their money into a string of motels.

One night a few months later the phone rings and you answer it. The call, you soon learn, is from the leader of an investment group. The group has three million dollars to put into motels. Would you be willing to join the group on an advisory basis without investing any capital but sharing equally in the profits?

Playing cool, using the soft sell, you say you'll have to think it over and check out your commitments. (Actually you'd be delighted to join the group because you recognize that this is your next BIG chance.)

Capitalize on Every Opportunity

You call back a few days later to say that you checked your schedule and find that you can spare them a few hours per week for advice and counsel. The group is delighted and they ask, "What's the next move?"

"I'll be back in touch in a day or two," you reply.

That same day you drop in to see your friend—the junior vice-president of your bank. "How are things going?" he asks.

"Great," you smile. "I'm now advising a group that has three million dollars to invest in motels. We're looking for a place to 'store' this money until we have it fully invested," you say casually.

He jumps up from his seat, saying "You just have to meet our senior vice-president *and* our president! Please come with me, *Sir*."

Within moments you're shaking hands with the senior vice-president and president in the latter's plush office. They're all practically bowing to you and fussing over you. "What can we do for you?" the president asks in a hopeful tone.

"Well, I'd like you to take care of the group's three million in cash until we find some suitable investments," you say.

"We'd be only too, too delighted," the president says excitedly.

"Then," you continue, "if we need any extra cash in the future, I'd be happy if you'd consider our loan application."

"Delighted to," the president replies, rubbing his hands in anticipation. "An account of this size gets my *personal* attention."

Be an Adviser—Hit the Big Money

You have the three million in funds transferred to your bank where it is deposited in the group's name. Then you begin searching for worthwhile motel investments. Only a few in the United States look interesting. You decide to go further afield.

So you try Western Europe, traveling through England, France, Belgium, Holland, Sweden, Denmark, Italy, and Germany with all your expenses paid by the group. During your trip you select four locations for spanking new motels and you take options on three existing motels. You return to the United States happy and ready for more action.

Accept Any Honest Pay

The group is so pleased with your work they vote you full ownership of one motel. This motel is worth $400,000, and you now control $300,-000 + $500,000 + $400,000 = $1,200,000 worth of property. You're delighted because your dream of great wealth is coming true.

Being an adviser has many advantages. It makes you

- An insider on many deals
- A good friend of every banker
- A companion of the wealthy
- A leader in your field

The next time you stop by at your bank the president rushes out to see you. "Don't you need another loan?" he asks.

"Yes, I might need fifty thousand or so," you say.

"Any time," he says. "Your credit is good up to a million. We'd be delighted to do business with you personally or with the group." He shakes your hand in a very friendly way.

The Million-Dollar Success Secret

Now just what did you do to corner all this wealth? You applied the *million-dollar success secret*. And what is that secret? Exactly this:

Borrow just enough money to control property or assets that will pay you an income large enough to pay off the loan and leave some cash for you. As soon as you're sure of making a profit from the first investment, take on another investment, using the assets of the first as collateral for your second loan.

Continue building this way until you reach your wealth goal. Within three years you should be able to control a million dollars in assets and have an income of $100,000 to $150,000 per year. What more could you ask for?

Is this million-dollar secret restricted to motels, real estate, and similar investments? No, not at all! You can apply the pyramiding technique to any business situation where the first loan yields income *and* assets of some kind—land, buildings, ships, stock, automobiles, etc. The key is to bring income and assets together to yield security and payoff for an additional loan.

Putting the Secret to Work

Earlier chapters in this book tell you:

- How to borrow money
- What to do to raise your credit rating
- Where to borrow the money you need

In this chapter you are learning how to get more than one loan at a time.

Many people, when I tell them about this technique during one of our conferences, ask: "Is it really honest to have more than one loan at a time?"

Certainly it is! Further, I would never recommend that you or anyone else ever do anything dishonest. It is easy enough to earn your fortune being honest—so why need anyone be dishonest?

Many large companies, and small ones as well, have a dozen loans outstanding at one time. Though I don't recommend that you aim at that large a number of loans, you shouldn't be afraid to have two or three outstanding at one time.

To put this million-dollar secret to work:

1. Choose an investment that appeals to you and provides income and assets.
2. Check the ads for the availability of the investment you want—if it is the type that is advertised.
3. Investigate at least six investments of the type you have in mind.
4. While you're investigating an investment, *observe, listen,* and *make notes.* Learn as much as you can about the type of investment that interests you. Knowledge is a source of power in business.
5. Determine what is the lowest down payment that will be accepted for an investment of the type you're considering.
6. Compare the lowest down payment required with the amount you could borrow on a personal signature-type loan.
7. If the required lowest down payment exceeds, by a few thousand dollars, the amount you can borrow, try to negotiate a lower down payment. The most the seller can do is say no—and there's always the possibility he'll say yes.
8. If the required lowest down payment is less than the maximum you can borrow, try to negotiate a lower down payment! You

can always use the cash you save. And if the owner says no, you still have more cash than you need.

9. Once you own the investment, build it up so it pays you the best income possible. Keep accurate records showing the exact income the business is paying you.

10. Keep looking for other business or investment possibilties. When you find a profitable one, repeat Steps 1 through 9, using the income and property as collateral for another loan.

11. Keep pyramiding loans and investments until you reach the income or net worth you desire.

Keep Searching—Never Give Up

Each year, during my business travels, I meet thousands of men and women in all kinds of businesses. Many of these people attend the lectures I conduct on improving business results and similar subjects.

Recently, at a lecture in London, England, an attendee asked: "Mr. Lecturer, what should someone who has failed in six different businesses do to change his luck?"

"Keep trying," I replied.

"But I do, and don't get any results," he shouted.

"Look at it this way," I said. "If you stop trying, you're positive you won't get any results. But if you keep trying, there's always the possibility you may hit it big." Then I told him the story of George K., a man who failed at everything but who nevertheless kept trying.

George K. reached his fiftieth birthday with little to show for his efforts. He had held various jobs during his life but none had paid very well. And the businesses he tried all failed.

One day, while riding to work on the subway, he was flooded with despair by a series of thoughts:

- All his life he had tried but failed
- There were so many things he wanted to do
- Time was rapidly passing him by
- If he didn't succeed soon he never would

George thought over his life and his business failures. Each failure, George discovered during his subway think session, had one common element: *He had approached the business directly without thinking of the benefits he, George K., would obtain.* Since that method hadn't paid off, i.e., he failed time after time, why not try another approach?

Notice George's thinking. He wasn't giving up. Instead, he was thinking of another way to keep trying! This brings us to our first rule for making *sure* you earn your fortune.

When you fail, try to analyze what went wrong, and why. Then try another approach. But never give up!

New Approaches Often Win

So George K. reversed his approach. Instead of listing what he would do in his next business, George listed what he would do with the profits from his next business *after* it was successful. Here are some of the items from his list:

- Learn to fly a small airplane
- Take a trip around the world
- Learn to dance well
- Buy a new Cadillac
- Take ski lessons

As you can see from this list, George wanted to do a number of things that many other people might also like to do—travel, fly, dance, etc.

Once he had his list of what he'd do *when* he had enough money, George added up the cost of these items. To his surprise, his total would be only about $100,000. That amount of money, George realized, was not an excessively large sum. But it certainly was more than he had now or ever had before. Thus George was facing his problem squarely. This brings us to our second rule:

Decide what you want from life. Then figure out a way to get what you want.

"That's the wrong approach," you say. "First get the money, then figure out what you want."

You are right—for some people. With others—like George and those folks who've had a series of failures—it's better for them to use their dreams of wealth, and what the money will give them to fuel their drive. For such folks, their wants:

- Spur them on to do more
- Make them more creative
- Lead to new methods of earning money
- Set up new success patterns

And, as you know, nothing succeeds like success. Once you get on the glorious road to wealth you will:

- Feel better
- Be much happier
- Have greater zest for life
- Develop new drive
- Earn more—faster

Knowing these facts, we can state our third rule:

Use your dream of wealth to stimulate yourself to money-earning action. Seek success in small things because one success builds another until great wealth is achieved.

Put Your Dreams into Action

George K. knew what he wanted. His only problem was how to get what he felt he'd like to have before he retired. Happily, George noted to himself, knowing what he wanted out of life gave him more drive than when he just had a general desire to earn more money. To get started, George made a list of what he could do to earn the money he needed. Here's his list.

- Buy a going company; build it up
- Invest in real estate
- Open a mail-order business
- Get a high-paying sales job

George studied his list. The more he looked at the list the clearer it became to George that he had to make money quickly. Waiting twenty years for his fortune was not at all attractive for a man in his fifties. For this reason, George was ready to put his dreams into action.

Plan Your Future Wealth

The future belongs to those who plan for it. This is particularly true in business because we can plan for the good *and* the bad. With proper plans we can prevent losses and be more certain of making gains.

George studied his chances of making a big fortune by buying a going business. The more he studied, the rosier the picture became because:

- A going company could be bought using borrowed money
- Loans could be pyramided to take over one company after another
- Earnings from the companies would repay the loans
- The company owner would receive his income from the company earnings
- When extra capital was needed a public stock issue could be made

George was ready to move ahead. But he moved slowly until he chanced to read of a young man who set a new record of acquiring wealth. In just six years this young man took over eight companies and, when he went public, wound up with stock worth $300 million.

George checked out a number of businesses, studying each for:

- Growth potential
- Capital required
- Manpower needs
- Competition in his area

Businesses that George considered included dry-cleaning, grocery stores, coin laundries, liquor stores, bowling alleys, book publishing, newspaper delivery routes, jewelry stores, and similar retail establishments. None appealed to him.

Next George turned to industrial businesses. These—such as machine shops, home renovating, building construction, electronic-equipment manufacture, etc.—also failed to interest him.

Watching Business Ads Helps

Just when he was about to give up, George saw an ad for a parking lot in his city. He realized immediately that this might be the answer to his business needs because

- Manpower requirements are small
- Growth potential is large
- Loans could be pyramided

George made an appointment to see the lot and its owner. The owner offered two deals to George. These were: (1) the lot could be rented on a monthly basis with a one-year lease; (2) the lot could be purchased outright with $5,000 cash down and a mortgage for the balance.

George decided to rent the lot for a year to see how well he did. "If the lot goes well," he promised himself, "I'll buy a nearby lot *and* this lot within a year."

George's plans worked out beautifully. He:

(1) Borrowed $3,000 on a personal loan for the one-year lot rental
(2) Had a man operate the parking lot for him
(3) Checked into the availability and prices of nearby parking lots
(4) Purchased, within six months, the first lot, and two others, using a personal loan for the down payment on each lot

Today George K. owns 14 parking lots in his city. His net income from each lot is $15,000 per year, giving a total net income of $210,000 per year. Thus, in a three-year period, George will have a total net income of more than half a million dollars. And this income is the sole result of:

- Loan pyramiding
- Careful study of opportunities
- Choice of an expandable business
- Low manpower needs

Make Your Business Build Itself

Recognize this key fact here and now:

As soon as you take over a going business your credit rating zooms. You may be deeply in debt but the fact that you own a business makes you a more desirable credit risk!

So even if you borrow the money to take over the business, you automatically, as a business owner, look better to a lender. "That's crazy," you say. Maybe it is, but it's a fact of business life that the more you owe the greater your potential growth.

Here's a typical growth plan used successfully by many Beginning Wealth Builders to make a business finance its own growth:

(1) Choose a suitable growth business
(2) Borrow money to take over the business
(3) Operate the business a short time
(4) Locate a second business for sale
(5) Use the first business as collateral for a loan
(6) Buy the second business using the loan obtained on the first business
(7) Continue this process until you have the income you desire

If you plan your moves well, you may be able to take over a business using OPM and walk away with extra cash! Plenty of BWBs do this regularly. Every time they walk away with extra cash they are making the business build itself by pyramiding loans. Here's a typical example:

- Your first business requires a down payment of, say, $5,000
- This first business pays off its loan ($160 per month for 36 months) *plus* its other expenses *and* gives you an income of $15,000 per year
- The income of the business increases under your careful operation
- When you need $10,000 to take over a second business, you use the first business as collateral and apply for a $15,000 loan
- The second or pyramided loan is quickly approved and you take over the second business with $10,000 of OPM while you pocket $5,000 of OPM. Thus, you're the owner of two businesses and have several thousand dollars in your pocket without putting a penny down!

Bank on the Future

When you pyramid loans you're banking on the future. To make sure this "bank" doesn't fail:

(1) Buy only going businesses—those that have established customers, a known income, and the possibility of future growth.

(2) The net income the business generates must pay you more than the sum of the monthly loan payment + any monthly payment to the seller + the monthly income you desire from the business.

(3) Before computing the monthly net income for a business be sure to deduct the cost of rent, light, heat, supplies, labor, etc.

(4) Insist on proof of income from the seller. Acceptable proof includes copies of past income-tax returns, sales receipts, and shipping bills of lading.

Now I want to warn you of one danger of this technique. That danger is:

When buying a business or taking over a service, be pessimistic! See things in their worst light. Use Murphy's law: "If something can go wrong, it will!"

Why do I, the person who's been urging you to have a positive mental attitude, suddenly switch and tell you to be pessimistic? Because when buying a business many people think only of the income they'll earn from the business. They seldom think of the income they may *not* earn when their customers go elsewhere.

So I urge you to look at both sides of every business situation. If the income meets the four tests above, fine. Then ask yourself:

(1) What would happen to me if the total income of the business fell to half of what I expect it to be?

(2) What would happen to the income if I couldn't get suitable employees?

(3) Could I feed customers from this business to another business if I were to buy a second business?

(4) Is the business I'm purchasing *really* profitable? Or am I just intrigued by some non-business factors such as location, atmosphere, an employee, etc.

(5) Do the records of the business reflect the seasonal variations such a business normally has? If the records don't reflect the normal variations, be careful. The records may be rigged.

Why jeopardize your future by not looking ahead? You can pyramid loans easily if you buy the right business and don't pay too much for it. Look upon a business as a vehicle to pay off the loan you take out to buy the business. With this outlook you'll soon clearly see that the main purpose of any business is to earn a profit for its owner. Without this approach to business, some people allow their emotions to get in the way of their judgement. This can be dangerous.

Build from One Loan to the Next

Clem F. wanted to make a fortune in a hurry without a lot of bother with a factory, payroll, overhead, and the other well-known problems of business. So Clem decided that he'd pick a business that didn't require more than a:

- Desk
- Telephone
- Supply of letter paper
- Few business leads

Clem F. checked into a large number of businesses and found that the business that best suited his needs was a licensing and new business organization for overseas firms. In such a business Clem would:

- License overseas firms to use American patents, processes, and similar industrial items
- License American firms to use overseas patents, processes, etc.
- Find new business for both American and overseas firms.

Clem would receive a fee, usually about 5 percent of the lump sum paid for use of a license. The license agreement would run for three to five years, with provision for renewal. On renewal of the license Clem would receive another 5 percent fee, plus a 1 percent bonus. Further, on some mass-production type licenses, Clem would receive a small royalty on each product made or sold.

Fees for finding new business might go as high as 10 percent, depending on the type of business, and other factors. A royalty payment would also be made in mass-production businesses.

The more Clem studied this licensing and acquisition business the more it interested him. Why? Because he'd need little more than a desk and telephone to run the business. At the start, he could even type his own letters and contracts! And he could get his leads from *International Wealth Success,* mentioned earlier in this book, and *Worldwide Riches Opportunities,* also mentioned.

Clem took out a $2,000 personal loan and opened his office. Within three months he was doing so well that he decided to open an overseas branch in London. So Clem went back to the bank and borrowed $5,000 more—this time as a business loan.

Using the same technique, Clem opened eight overseas offices. Today Clem's take-home pay is nearly $200,000 per year. "If it weren't for loan pyramiding I'd still be without a secretary," Clem laughs. Currently Clem has four secretaries.

What are other, similar businesses you might build up quickly with pyramided loans? Here are a number:

- Manufacturer's representative
- Talent agent
- Travel bureau
- Real estate broker
- Business or industrial consultant
- Inventor or patent developer

Local pyramiding can be *your* way to great wealth. Put the hints in this chapter to work and watch your fortune grow and grow!

13

Easy Ways to Pay Off Your Loans

Borrowing money is lots of fun—many people consider borrowing a game in which they match wits with the lender. But like any other fun in life, we eventually have to repay—and in the borrowing game we must put money on the line. And sometimes repaying money is not as easy or as pleasant as receiving money. In this chapter I hope to show you how to pay and grin.

Know Your Payoff Limits

All of us have two kinds of loan payoff limits. They are:

- Financial
- Mental

The financial payoff limit is understood by most folks. Put simply, the financial payoff limit says:

Don't take on a fixed debt repayment obligation which is greater than your ability to repay.

Thus, the businessman who takes on a $200-per-month loan repayment obligation when he can afford to repay only $100 per month is asking for trouble. As a general guide, I recommend to Beginning Wealth Builders (BWBs) that:

When borrowing business funds never take on a fixed loan repayment obligation which is more than half the amount you can afford to pay.

This means that if you can afford to repay $500 per month, you shouldn't take on a repayment of more than $250 per month. Why the difference? To give you a cushion, in case something goes wrong. Once you acquire some solid business experience, you may want to cut your margin a little thinner—borrow right up to your limit to repay. That's okay—when you know what you're doing.

Recognize Your Mental Payoff Limits

The second payoff limit is one that few people recognize when they first borrow money. It is what I call a *mental payoff limit*:

Many people can make loan repayments for only a certain number of months; then they become restless and want to get rid of the need to make repayments.

Over the years I have watched many BWBs, as well as myself, as loans were repaid. Many of these BWBs get itchy at certain times during the loan payoff period, if it exceeds 18 months. Why is this?

Well, a year is a relatively short time. If your loan repayment period runs 12 months, you repay the loan quickly and easily. Your period of pain is over before you know it.

Some Loans Are Easier Than Others

Much the same is true of an 18-month loan. Eighteen months is just a little more than a year. So before you have time to weary of loan payments you're sending in the last check.

But when your loan period runs 24, 36, 48, or 60 months, there's plenty of time to get weary of those payments. I personally become tired after about 22 months. All I can think of is getting rid of the payment.

Some BWBs have more patience. They don't get tired until their thirty-third payment. Great! They'll build a big fortune.

Now don't worry about your mental payoff period. It won't get you into trouble—it will just make you itchy to unload your business debt. If you want to, you can use this desire as a source of motivation to pay off your loan sooner. How? Here are several useful techniques.

- Double your monthly payment—this will halve the payoff time remaining while presenting you with a real challenge to earn the money you need for the double payment.

- Pay off your loan in one payment using funds you accumulated in your business. This saves you interest costs and gets rid of your mental payoff burden.
- Borrow enough money to pay off the balance of your current loan. "That's crazy," you say. "You're just replacing one loan with another." True, but the new loan seems less of a burden than the old one. Further, you may be able to gain a few months' no-payment grace if your second loan is the type where you make no payments for the first three months (personal signature-type loans are often of this kind).

Pace Yourself for Loan Repayments

Business loans *must* eventually be repaid. A *term loan* may allow you to go for a year with only interest payments. But at the end of the year you must *renew* the loan; i.e., either pay it off by repaying the lender the principal or by signing a new note and paying the interest, in advance, for the next year. Either way, you must *pace* yourself—by that I mean prepare yourself mentally and financially—to a repayment cycle.

Sometimes you may find that repaying a loan is brutally difficult. By that I mean that you must scratch and scrounge for the money for every payment. You find every payment a painful struggle, not because you're avoiding payment but because you have fewer dollars than you need.

Other loans will seem like a breeze to you. The monthly or annual payment is so small you can easily handle it. To speed up your repayments you occasionally double or triple a payment when you have a few extra dollars.

Four Powerful Repayment Techniques

But to pace yourself for those difficult, painful loans which I'm almost certain you'll have, here are four powerful repayment techniques:

(1) Recognize that every business loan *must* be repaid. Why? Because if you ever fail to repay a business loan your credit rating will be ruined for years—perhaps for life.

(2) Mentally see yourself making monthly or annual repayments on your loan *before* you receive the money. Get in tune to make your payments *on time*.

(3) Make one or two *advance* payments when you receive your loan, if the loan is the monthly repayment type. These advance payments will give you a cushion against a lean income month now and then.

(4) Save an amount equal to three monthly payments, as soon as you can. Keep this money ready to use for a payment now and then when your income is down. As soon as you use a portion of this fund, start saving again to replace it so you always have at least a three-month reserve.

Make Your Loan Payments First

Gear yourself to paying off your loan by making your first payment each month your loan repayment. Repeat to yourself, ten times every day: *Do it now.* This will build up a positive pay-off-the-loan attitude. You'll find that any tendency you might have had to procrastinate will quickly disappear.

Kathy C. works in Wall Street. One day, while joking with a highly reputable stock broker, she asked him: "What stock would you recommend to a cautious single girl like me?"

"Buy as much as you can of XYZ," he replied. "You can pick it up at sixty cents a share right now."

That was in April. Kathy didn't have a dime in the bank. But she trusted the broker. So she took out a $5,000 signature loan to buy clothing and consolidate some debts she had. But after spending some of the loan on these things, Kathy changed her mind, as any woman or man is entitled to, and decided to invest the balance in XYZ stock. By this time XYZ had risen to seventy cents a share. Kathy bought 6,000 shares for a little more than $4,200, the amount she had left over from the loan.

Stick with Your Beliefs

Kathy will never forget *that* summer on Wall Street. It was the hottest summer in recent years and her temperature seemed to rise with the price of XYZ. First it hit a dollar a share; then two dollars. When the price reached ten dollars a share, Kathy excitedly called her broker friend. "What should I do?" she wailed.

"Don't do a thing—just hang on until you hear from me," he laughed. "XYZ is going a lot higher. Don't let the heat get you!"

Kathy took his advice and hung on until fall, by which time XYZ was up to $28 per share. Once again she called the broker. "I told you to sit tight," he said, somewhat annoyed.

Meanwhile, Kathy kept repeating: *Do it now*. And each month she made a payment on her loan *before* anything else—rent, electricity, gas, etc.

Finally, in December, the broker called. "XYZ is at 34, Kathy. Sell now!"

Kathy immediately sold her 6,000 shares at $34 each, receiving $204,-000. After paying off her loan and brokerage fees, Kathy had nearly $200,000. That's not bad for an eight-month investment of OPM!

Keep the Faith in Your Loan

Now not everyone who makes his loan payments before any other payment will have Kathy's luck. But:

Making your loan payment first keeps your business needs foremost in your thoughts. This will help you become more successful, sooner.

Never give up your faith in the magic power of OPM. Lenny M. found this out—to his great delight—just as he was about to give up in his attempt to earn a big fortune.

Personal Loans Can Pay Off Big

Lenny took out four personal loans to buy some property in San Juan, Puerto Rico. The property was in an area that was being rapidly built up and Lenny hoped to sell the land in a quick deal. But Lenny overlooked two items when he took out the loans:

(1) The property wasn't generating any income to pay off the loans.
(2) The property was loaded with squatters who were difficult to remove.

So Lenny had two problems. One—how to pay off the loans—was an immediate problem. The other—how to get rid of the squatters—was a longer range problem. But he couldn't turn his land into profitable cash until he solved the squatter problem. So the sooner he solved it, the earlier he could make big money.

The longer Lenny pondered his problem the more convinced he became that there was only one way out of his predicament. This was:

Take out another loan and use it to make the initial payments on the existing loans. This loan would "buy time"—prolong the period available for finding a solution to the problem.

In short, Lenny was keeping the faith in his original loans and using the new loan to buy some time. Further, the new loan would act as an incentive by pushing Lenny into finding a solution for the problem (the squatters) that forced him to take out the new loan.

Work Fast—Don't Waste Time

Lenny's big problem now was that of getting rid of the squatters. Squatters the world over have a reputation for being stubborn, determined, and crafty people. They have to be if they are to get along in a world where they take the land that appeals to them. So Lenny's problem of getting rid of his squatters wasn't easy.

Lenny sensed, however, that if he worked fast he might be more successful than if he spent a long time talking and negotiating with the squatters. The question was: What's the best way to get rid of the squatters?

Lenny sat down and looked at the problem from the squatters' viewpoint. To be induced to move from their rent-free shacks the squatters must be offered:

(1) Rent-free or very-low-rent quarters
(2) Much more attractive quarters
(3) Free moving
(4) Protection from prosecution

Lenny checked out some nearby low-cost housing. He found that for only a few hundred dollars he could move, and pay the first year's rent, for the squatters on his property. He went to them with his plan. After a short discussion the squatters gladly accepted Lenny's offer.

As soon as he had the squatters off the land, Lenny put the property up for sale. Within two weeks he sold it at a profit of $18,000, after deducting the cost of moving the squatters. Quick action paid off handsomely.

Get Quick Magic Results

Why do I recommend working fast? Because

Most business deals move slowly; when you take fast action you gain the respect and admiration of your associates. This allows you to get more done in less time.

As soon as Lenny received the money for his land he paid off the five loans he'd taken out to pay for the land. This saved him interest and zoomed his reputation with his bankers. "Come back again," they all said. "We'd be delighted to do business with you."

People everywhere love a winner. You can be a winner if you work fast in every business deal. Why spend 30 years trying to make a fortune when you can make almost as much in three years by working fast?

Start with a Positive Payoff Plan

You'll feel nervous the first time you take out a business loan. But you needn't be the slightest bit nervous if you have a positive payoff plan. What kind of a plan is this? A positive payoff plan is one which:

(1) Recognizes your payoff limits
(2) Prepares for potential problems
(3) Shows, in writing, the payoff sequence
(4) Readies you for future loans

Let's take a look at each of these elements of a positive payoff plan, except the first, which we discussed at the start of this chapter.

Prepare for potential problems: This technique is often called PPA—potential problem analysis. To prepare for potential problems:

Look ahead to see what could go wrong with your business loan. Take action now to prevent these problems, before they occur.

Analyze your problems in writing. Don't rely on your head alone. With your problems written out, you'll see aspects that wouldn't occur to you when analyzing your potential problems mentally.

Show, in writing, the payoff sequence: Plan ahead, in writing. If you take out a 36-month loan, list on a sheet of paper the numbers 1 through 36. Beneath each number, list the amount of money you plan to pay the lender that month.

"I'll just make one payment each month," you say. "So why go to the trouble of making such a list?"

There are plenty of reasons. If your business prospers, as it should, you'll start doubling up your payments during the second year. By this I mean that instead of making single payments during the second year, you'll make two payments at once. This means you'll pay off your loan in 24 months instead of 36 months.

And here's another valuable hint that will help you pay off your loan faster:

Each month, when you make a payment, check it off on your list. The thrill of seeing the number of remaining payments go down will spur you on.

Keep Your Enthusiasm High

The biggest and most important secret of people who build enormous fortunes is their great enthusiasm for business and the wealth it brings them. Most people fail to hit the big money in business because:

- Their enthusiasm is short-lived
- They don't plan their wealth efforts
- They hop from one idea to another
- They give up too soon

Build *your* enthusiasm for a larger income. Why? Because being enthusiastic will:

- Improve your wealth chances
- Increase your happiness
- Improve your mental outlook
- Help you pay off loans faster

Adopt a positive mental attitude towards your life. You *can* and *will* build the wealth you want if you believe you can. Without a strong belief in yourself, and enthusiasm to power your daily efforts, you have little chance of hitting the big money.

Be Creative About Payoff Schemes

I could spend the remainder of this book suggesting different kinds of loan payoff schemes. Yet the best payoff schemes for you are the ones you develop yourself. Why? Because:

When you're creative about loan payoff methods you become more creative in other areas of your business life. This can zoom your income.

Here, as a source of ideas for you, are a number of useful loan payoff schemes. Look them over for possible ideas that may be useful in your business deals.

Use These 12 Sure-Fire Payoff Methods

To pay off your business loans, use these 12 wealth-laden techniques:

- Double or triple your payments whenever you have extra income.
- When you take out a loan, request double the amount you need. Use half the money received for your business and the other half as capital to repay half your loan. By the time you run out of borrowed capital, your business should be earning enough to begin repaying the balance of your loan.
- When you're paying on several loans at once, take out a loan which is large enough to pay off all the small loans. Pay them off; then concentrate on paying off the bigger, more important loans.
- Take out a "three-month delay loan" for the amount you need. With this type of loan you needn't make any payments for three months after you receive the money. During these three months you can put the money to work in your business.
- Use any collateral your business produces (such as valuable equipment, stocks, bonds, etc.) as a source of new loans or to convert a monthly-payment loan to a demand loan—a loan on which you make payments whenever you wish.
- Accumulate cash from your business until you have enough to pay off your loan in one shot.
- Or, if you wish, use your accumulated business cash as a compensating balance and take out a loan to pay off your existing loan or loans.
- Find a means of converting a fixed-payment loan to a non-fixed-payment loan. This means you can use compensating balance, collateral, renegotiation to a term loan, etc.
- Sell part of the assets—such as equipment, customer lists, or accounts—which you obtain when you purchase a business. Use the money received to pay off part, or all, of the loans you took out to buy the business.
- Mortgage—take out a loan on—the assets you obtain when you purchase a business. Use the money received to pay off the loan used to buy the business.
- Go public by selling stock in your company. Use part of the proceeds from the public offering to pay off the loan used to buy your business.
- Use your business income to set up a revolving credit account at two or more banks. Withdraw some money from each account to pay off any loans you now have outstanding.

Get to Know Your Lender

Jerry C. borrowed $10,000 to buy an indoor swimming pool near his home. The pool was in good condition but the ladies' and mens' locker rooms were run down. So was the exterior of the building housing the pool. But worst of all, the income from the business was at a low level.

Jerry believed he could build up the business, once he could improve the outside appearance and the locker rooms.

To know exactly where he was headed, Jerry sat down and listed his plans for building up the business. Since he needed customers, and as many as he could get, Jerry decided to offer attractive discounts to large groups, including:

Boy Scouts	Women's clubs
Girl Scouts	Fraternal groups
Sea Scouts	Religious groups

Jerry figured the cost of repainting the exterior and rebuilding the interior of the locker rooms. The work would cost about $5,000. Since Jerry was already financed up to the hilt, he was at a loss as to what to do next.

On an impulse one day, Jerry decided to call the loan officer at the bank where he obtained the original $10,000 loan. The loan officer was extremely friendly. After an exchange of a few remarks, Jerry said, "I'll be downtown at lunch time—how about having a quick lunch together."

"Sure," the loan officer replied. "I'll be looking for you at about noon."

Bankers Are Human, Too

At lunch, Jerry soon learned that the loan officer:

- Enjoyed swimming
- Had a son in the Boy Scouts
- Wanted to encourage youthful sports

As soon as Jerry learned these facts about the loan officer, he told him about his plan to improve the pool. "Do you need any money to do the improvement work?" the loan officer asked.

"Yes, $5,000," Jerry said.

"Oh, we can get that for you in a few minutes," the banker said. "Money like that is no problem."

Jerry and the loan officer finished lunch and returned to the bank. The loan officer had Jerry fill out a short application giving details of the loan. An hour later Jerry received a $5,000 check which he deposited in his account.

Today Jerry's indoor pool is a booming business. Youth and adult groups from all over the area regularly swim in the pool. And what is Jerry doing? He's looking for another pool to take over.

Pyramid Your Business Interests

During recent years you've probably watched with interest the growth of the conglomerates—those large firms composed of many smaller firms in a variety of businesses. And you've probably noted the great fortunes that the founders of many of these conglomerates built in a few years. Did you ever ask yourself—"Why couldn't I do the same?"

Well, you can—even though you start smaller and grow at a slower rate. How can you build your own conglomerate? It's easy, if you follow these five steps:

(1) Borrow enough money to buy a business of your choice.
(2) Operate the business for six months to a year and accumulate as much cash as possible.
(3) While operating the first business, look around for another business to take over.
(4) Use the cash from the first business, another loan, or stock sold to the public, to finance purchase of the second business.
(5) Continue making similar take-overs until you have as many businesses as you want.

Allow Synergy to Take Charge

Synergy is a recently discovered concept which states:

The results obtained by two or more creative groups working together is greater than the sum of their individual efforts.

This means that when you take the resources, manpower, and know-how of two or more businesses and bring them together, the results you'll obtain can be greater than what you'd obtain from each company working on its own.

Let's say, for instance, that you take over three companies—A, B, and C. The net income of these companies is:

Company	Annual net income
A	$12,000
B	25,000
C	18,000
Total	$55,000

When you combine these three firms

* Their managements work together
* Savings result from combining certain service departments—accounting, payroll, etc.
* Creative ideas are exchanged and used in each business

Now what does synergy have to do with your paying off business loans? Just this:

When synergy works for you—as it will in any well-planned conglomerate—the synergistic effect you obtain can pay off every loan you took out to buy the businesses!

Thus, Joe L. started his mini-conglomerate with a gas station which he took over using $3,000 of borrowed OPM. Once Joe had the gas station under good control and producing a profit, he began to look around for other businesses he could take over with only a small amount of cash.

Soon Joe had a real-estate office, a pet shop, a hardware store, a second gas station, and a laundry. His net income from these businesses was $75,000 the first year. And when synergy went to work during the second year, Joe's income topped $100,000. And all of this resulted from an investment of only $3,000 of borrowed OPM!

Use Investment Income to Pay Off Loans

Sometimes you'll be better off investing some of the cash income from your business instead of using it all to pay off loans. When you do this, the income from your investment will help pay off your loan. Here's a good example of how this can work.

Charles M. owed money on several loans after he took over two businesses. With a good cash flow into his businesses, Charles considered doubling or tripling his monthly loan payments. But before doing this he decided to look around to see if there was a better way to put his cash to work.

During his looking Charles heard of a highly successful small computer software company that was going public. Its shares were being offered to the public at $7.50 each.

Charles called the company and they referred him to their broker. Since computer-company stocks were booming at this time, Charles ordered 700 shares of stock. At $7.50 per share his cost was $5,250 plus commission.

Within one week the stock rose to $30 per share. Charles sold the 700 shares for $21,000, less commissions and transfer tax. His profit in one week was thus nearly $21,000 − 5,250 = $15,750. Charles used this profit to clear up all the loans on his businesses. This example brings out an important concept:

Sometimes you can profit more by investing extra cash than by paying off a loan with this cash. But before using this approach, be certain you know what you're doing in terms of your investment.

Note that you needn't depend just on the growth of the value of an investment to pay off a loan. You can also use:

- Dividend income
- Interest income
- Capital-gains income
- Any other kind of income

The major objective, regardless of the name of the income, is to pay off your loans.

Tap Foreign Money Sources

At times the United States of America is the most maligned and most criticized country in the world. Yet, as I travel throughout the world on various business matters, I note with delight that people everywhere love American:

- Autos, trucks, buses
- Chewing gum, chocolate bars
- Cigarettes, cigars
- Stocks, bonds
- Aircraft, pleasure boats

What does all this interest and willingness to purchase mean to you when you must meet a monthly loan payment? Plenty. Why? Because:

If you have a going business you may be able to sell shares in your firm to overseas investors.

Thus, a real-estate firm organized an international trust to sell shares
of its stock overseas. The income from the sale will be used to pay for
real estate—buildings such as apartments, factories and offices, and land
—in the United States. The trust is selling one million shares of stock at
$10 per share. This will produce a cash reserve of some $10 million
within a short time—less than three months. There aren't many outstanding loans larger than $10 million.

For leads on overseas brokers, agents, sales representatives, and deal-
ers who could be helpful to you, be sure to read the monthly newsletter
International Wealth Success.

You *can* pay off your loans quickly and easily. Just follow the many
hints in this chapter. Or use these hints as a source of ideas which you
develop especially for your debt situation.

Useful Loan Payoff Reading

At the end of the next chapter you'll find a list of helpful books which
may give you other ideas on how to pay off your loan. I suggest that
you look these books over and buy those that appear to be useful. *Remember:* One good idea from just one book can make you a fortune.
Every penny you invest in good business books is money that is well
invested.

14

Build Your Loans
to a Great Fortune

OPM—other people's money—is of little use to you unless you put it to work earning money for yourself. To borrow money and not put it to work is a waste of time and energy. That's why I'm devoting this chapter to showing you useful and positive techniques for building your loans to a great fortune.

Be Alert for Opportunities

You must be alert for wealth opportunities around you or that come your way. Why? Because:

It is usually easier to borrow OPM (if you use the methods given in this book) than it is to find good opportunities to make a big fortune.

So be alert at all times. Here are six profitable ways to find more wealth-building opportunities in your life.
(1) Read a good, big-city newspaper every day. Pay particular attention to the financial pages and business ads.
(2) Talk to businessmen everywhere. Start the conversation—but then allow the businessman to take over. Remember: "You ain't learin' when your tongue is turnin'."
(3) Listen to conversations you overhear on planes, trains, buses, in restaurants, etc. You'll often pick up valuable pieces of information. Also, you'll learn that many business problems other people have are often similar to your own.

(4) Read widely. At the front of this book you'll find a list of the titles of the three other business books written by this author for his present publisher. In full humility, I think that all three of these books might be of some help to you. So I suggest you buy all three. Close to a million other people have read the three books and praised their content. Naturally, there are many other good business books. I've listed a number of them at the end of this chapter.

(5) Read good business publications—*The Wall Street Journal, International Wealth Success, Barron's Magazine, Fortune,* etc. Be alert at all times while reading these publications. You never know when a fortune-building idea will hit you.

(6) Think; think; think. Nothing replaces thinking—*your* thinking. Your mind is unique—you have an approach to problems different from every other person in this world. So start thinking right now —and keep thinking every minute of the day and night. One right, bright idea could make you rich forever.

Seek and You Shall Find

Clyde R. wanted to speculate in real estate. Yet the largest amount of money he could borrow—$5,000 on a personal signature loan—was too small to allow Clyde to take over more than one property. But Clyde wanted to take over a number of properties. Clyde believed that his greatest profit potential was in a setup where he had a number of properties to operate.

"Be as alert as possible," I told Clyde when he mentioned his problem. "Read everything you can that will be of any help to you."

Clyde did as I recommended. One day he came across an obscure small-type ad in his local paper. The ad announced a sheriff's sale of some real-estate properties to the highest bidder.

Clyde attended the sale and several others in the next few weeks. At these sales Clyde saw:

- A split-level home having a market value of $23,500 sold for $180.22
- A 27-room mansion on 13 waterfront acres sold for $96.18
- A $12,000 farm-style home sold for $555.32

While none of these properties were completely free and clear of mortgages, Clyde realized that if he purchased anv of them he could:

- Re-sell the property at a profit
- Rent the property at a profit
- Merge the property with other parcels

The important point is that Clyde found a way to take over numerous real-estate properties with the amount of money he could borrow—$5,000. His alertness paid off.

Establish Your Own Business

As soon as Clyde discovered, and analyzed, the gold available in sheriff's forced sales of property, he formed his own real estate business. Immediately thereafter Clyde began buying real estate offered at sheriff's sales. Once he acquired a property, Clyde would try to:

- Sell the property back to the original owner at a profit
- Sell the property to a new buyer at a profit
- Rent the property to cover costs and show a profit

Using this technique, Clyde purchased and sold some 25 properties in a six-month period. His profit on these deals was $68,000. After repaying the $5,000 loan, Clyde walked away with a $63,000 profit. This is a neat profit for six months of part-time work!

You Can Make Big Money Now

"He has a special gimmick—the sheriff's sales," you say.

That may be so. But every town and city in America has either a sheriff's sale, or its equivalent. So you, too, can have *your* special gimmick in *your* area. And since almost anyone can borrow $5,000 using a personal signature loan, you can easily hit the big money right now—if real estate interests you.

If you are the type of person who likes other businesses better—say retail sales, consulting, or product servicing—you can still make big money using only a small amount of borrowed capital.

How? Be alert. Look, every day of the week, for unusual opportunities. These chances *do* exist. All you have to do is find them.

"Clyde was just lucky," someone says.

Perhaps. But whenever I hear such a remark I think of a good friend of mine—a man who is worth more than $100 million. Yet he started with nothing except a driving urge to make a fortune. He often remarks:

"When someone tells you another man earned his money because he was lucky, just remember this: Luck comes to those who are ready for it —those who studied, worked, and prepared to be lucky! So the next time someone says 'Oh, he was just lucky,' remind them that getting ready to be lucky takes work!"

So you, too, can be lucky—if you get ready now. I am firmly convinced that if you prepare well, luck will find you. Then people will say about you: "He was the right man in the right place at the right time." Being ready when the call comes gives you more advantages than you ever thought possible. And, as Ben Franklin sagely observed, "Money makes money. And its offspring begets more."

Never Become Discouraged

Business, like life, has its ups and downs. Some days may be better and more profitable than others. But to have the profitable days you must also, generally, have the less profitable days.

Never become discouraged. Keep working and trying at all times. Even on an unprofitable day the experience you gain may be just what you need to make your fortune the next day.

Be careful of critics—people who tell you that:

- You're wasting your time
- You don't know what you're doing
- You'll fail miserably
- You're going ahead at the wrong time

Critics are the cheapest unwanted business commodity in the world. Most critics are empty-headed eavesdroppers. They just can't refrain from injecting themselves into other people's activities.

Use Money Goals

Set up, stick with, and achieve your money goals. Using goals has many advantages for you. Money goals

- Give you a specific target to aim for
- Pace your fortune-building efforts
- Provide a time deadline
- Allow you to measure your progress
- Help you correct mistakes

Every big business uses goals to guide its efforts. Your business—no matter how small it may be—is big business to you. So follow the pattern of successful big businesses and:

- Set up your money goals
- Work towards these goals
- Make sure you achieve your goals

Money goals can be the high-test fuel that powers your drive towards great riches. Recognize this now and you'll outdistance your competitors quickly and easily.

Put Numbers on Your Goals

Money goals without numbers on them are almost useless. Compare these two goals:

- I'd like to be really rich.
- I plan to be worth $500,000 three years from now.

The first goal is indefinite—it doesn't define *how much* money is wanted, or the *date* when this money is wanted.

The second goal, by contrast, tells how much, and when. With such a goal it is easy for the beginning wealth builder (BWB) to check his progress.

Use the Milestone Technique

As some of my readers know, I began my career as an engineer. So it was only natural for me to use some engineering methods in my wealth building. Thus far, these methods have been highly successful for me and for hundreds of people I've advised. One of these methods is called the milestone technique.

In the milestone technique you set up check points called *milestones* to monitor and control your progress toward your goal. The milestone technique tells you where you stand every week, month, quarter, or for whatever other interval you choose.

The major advantage of the milestone technique is that it

- Forces you to set up check points
- Requires you to check where you stand
- Allows you to take action quickly

Avoid Beginners' Mistakes

Most BWBs manage to make money with few serious mistakes. Why? Because they're so interested in their business activities that they pay constant attention to them. Those BWBs who do make mistakes usually don't:

- Have specific money goals
- Plan their wealth program
- Look at the condition of their business

Many BWBs understand the first two items. But the last gives them trouble because it means taking time away from making money. Yet if you are to hit the really big money you must:

- Compare actual income vs. planned income
- Raise your money goals as time passes
- Know where you stand in your plan

I've seen large companies get into serious trouble and small businessmen go broke simply because they didn't look at their financial plans often enough. Result? They didn't know where they stood. And before they knew it they had money problems. Any action they took was too late. Remember:

When you review your business situation at regular intervals you catch troubles while they're still small and you can do something about them. This prevents little problems from becoming big problems.

Control Your Future

That's where the milestone technique comes into play. To use the milestone technique, you set up a series of specific events which must occur on your path to wealth. Alongside each event you list the date on which you expect this event to occur. Here's a list of events prepared by a BWB who built a quick fortune in real estate.

Event	Date
1. Get loan application	9/1
2. Fill out application	9/2
3. Present application to bank	9/3
4. Obtain loan approval	9/4

5.	Deposit loan check	9/5
6.	Allow check to clear	9/15
7.	Verify check clearance	9/16
8.	Make down payment on property	9/18
9.	Close property purchase	9/28
10.	Advertise property for sale	10/10
11.	Repeat ad, if not sold	10/20
12.	Sell property	11/1
13.	Pay off loan	12/1

If you want, you can plot these milestones on a horizontal bar chart. Thus, the milestones related to your loan—numbers 1 through 4—would be plotted on one horizontal bar. Next, a second horizontal bar could be used to plot the check deposit and clearance milestones, numbers 5, 6, and 7. The property purchase, items 8 and 9, could be shown on a third bar. When finished, your chart would contain a series of horizontal bars having two or more dates on them. Each date is a milestone on your path to wealth.

Now if something goes wrong—say a problem with the property deed—your next milestone on your chart immediately alerts you. So you take action on the problem instantly—without wasting time. The milestone chart becomes particularly valuable as the number of projects you're working on increases. Once again:

The more often you look at a business deal, the better your chances for detecting trouble before it becomes serious.

Make Use of Friends

Your friends can help you earn more money—if these friends know business and how the businessman's mind works. Some of my best deals have been made through friends—yet I often hadn't known these friends more than a few months. "Then why do you call them friends?" you ask.

Because when two *true* businessmen get together they understand each other within minutes. This is true regardless of the differences in their businesses. The profit motive is the same all over the world—yes, even in the U.S.S.R. So no matter where you go or what business you may be in, you can find a friend.

Develop New Ideas

A friend of mine started a small business in his spare time. Within five years his business grew to the point where it was worth $600 million.

"Fantastic," you say. "How could any business grow that fast. Do you realize that's an average growth of 100 million dollars per year!"

Yes, I realize that. And I'm *not* putting you on. This is a true incident. The company is still going strong today, growing as rapidly as ever.

"Then how do you explain this type of growth?" you ask.

That's simple—*he developed a new idea into a saleable product*. New ideas—your new ideas—can be a gold mine. But you must:

(1) Actively seek really *new* ideas

(2) Develop worthwhile ideas into saleable items

(3) Keep up a steady flow of new ideas

One good new idea can be worth half a billion dollars to you, as it was to my friend.

"What business was his idea in?" you ask.

The computer field. And as you know, this is one of the fastest growing fields in the world today.

Let Others Develop Your Ideas

Let's say that you're an *idea type;* that is, you like to generate ideas, but developing them into marketable products doesn't interest you. What should you do?

That's easy. Get someone else to develop your ideas. There are many firms that will do this for you for no charge, provided you give them a share of the profits. You'll find many of these firms listed in *International Wealth Success,* the newsletter mentioned earlier in this book.

Expand Your Overseas Business

In the United States we have less than 10 percent of the world's population. That means that 90 percent of the market for any product—in terms of the number of people who might want it—is outside the United States. To any businessman these facts clearly indicate one conclusion.

To be successful today, you must study, and consider, the overseas market. Further, the chances are good that you'll find a lucrative overseas market for your product.

What might you sell overseas? Almost any item having a domestic market also has an overseas market. For valuable information about doing business overseas, refer to the book *Worldwide Riches Opportunities: 2500 Great Leads for Making Your Fortune in Overseas Trade Without Leaving Home.* This useful book lists the names and addresses of thousands of overseas firms throughout the world that want to buy hundreds of thousands of different U. S. products. Also listed are hundreds of overseas firms offering saleable imports to U. S. firms, and hundreds of other overseas firms wanting to be your overseas sales representative. To obtain a copy, send $25 to IWS, P. O. Box 186, Merrick, N. Y. 11566. You'll find the information well worth the price if you want to do business overseas.

How can you do business overseas from your own home? That's easy. You can:

(1) Locate, using the above book, overseas firms seeking products made in the U. S. After finding one or more such overseas firm, contact U. S. firms making the products wanted. Arrange the deal and take a 5 to 10 percent, or larger commission.

(2) Find overseas sales representatives for U. S. companies. Become an agent for the U. S. company and take a commission on every sale you make to your overseas sales rep. *Or,* arrange for direct contact between the U. S. company and the overseas sales rep and take a commission on all sales.

(3) Locate saleable imports for U. S. companies. Arrange the deal and take a commission from both the U. S. buyer and the overseas seller.

Earn Big Money While You Sleep!

European time is five to eight hours ahead of United States' time, depending on your location. So if you work out overseas sales or business arrangements with one or more European firms, you can be earning money while you sleep! Here's how.

Your European agent starts work at 9 A.M. Depending on your location in the United States, the time in your area will be between 1 A.M. and 5 A.M. If you're like most other people, you'll be sleeping while your European agent is working for you.

So check into the possibility of doing business overseas. With a copy of *Worldwide Riches Opportunities* on hand, all you need is a typewriter and some letter paper. Using your ingenuity and common sense, you should be able to earn a good income working right in your own living room. In fact, some people start on their kitchen table! Remember this:

When you work out mail-order arrangements with overseas agents or companies, the location where you do the work is unimportant— what counts is the results!

Another advantage of expanding your overseas business is that you can, if you wish, travel to visit your foreign contacts. This travel is a legitimate business expense and is deductible as such on your income tax return. This means you travel free of charge—the business pays your expenses.

Keep Your Investment Low

Just the fact that you can borrow, let's say, $5,000 on your signature, is no reason for investing every penny of it in your business. A better approach is to invest a portion of the money and keep the balance on hand for emergencies. What's more:

The smaller your investment, the harder you'll work, and the greater your chances for success.

Now a business based on your bringing together overseas and American business needs can require only a few dollars in cash. Yet the profit potential is enormous.

Gus K. started an overseas product search and licensing business with $300 of borrowed capital. Using lists such as those contained in *Worldwide Riches Opportunities,* Gus was able to expand his income from zero to one million dollars in just four years. During that time Gus made 32 trips overseas. Since he enjoys traveling, the trips were not a burden to him.

"I could still have made big money if I stayed home," Gus says. "But I made more, and had more fun, by traveling."

You may need more than Gus did to get started in your overseas business. Or you may need less. Much depends on how elaborate an organization you want to start with. If you're satisfied with a small, one-man or one-woman firm with a part-time secretary, you can get started with $500, or less.

Make Your Hobbies Pay Off

There's nothing as enjoyable as a profitable hobby. Why? Because you can have fun while you earn money! As some of you who have read my three other fortune-building books know, I have made my boating hobby a profitable income source. You can do the same with your hobby—be it hunting, skiing, fishing, travel, bowling, or anything else.

Joe J. flies a light airplane as his hobby. In recent years Joe noticed a big increase in interest, amongst private pilots, in vintage aircraft—airplanes from World War I, World War II, etc. Planes that once were sold for scrap for $100 today bring as high as $50,000 each in the used plane market. After hearing this, Joe J. decided to get in on the big money.

Plan for Great Success

During the long winter evenings Joe sat by his fireside and pondered the problem: Where can I get old fighter, bomber, and observation aircraft to sell? One evening the answer came in a flash—go where the great air battles occurred.

For the next several months Joe J. studied the air history of World War II. The more he read the more convinced he became that the uninhabited islands of the South Pacific might contain some abandoned military airplanes. Joe decided to borrow $2,000 and spend his next vacation flying over the small and large islands in a light plane to locate the planes he knew would bring him big profits.

Taking a commercial flight to Manila, in the Phillipines, Joe was soon exploring, from the air, many historic battle sites. By the second week Joe was in the out-islands. And it was during the second week that Joe made his big finds—two P-38s in almost-new condition tucked away in the jungle, a crashed but repairable Japanese Zero, and a crashed but only slightly damaged P-39.

Returning to Manila, Joe borrowed $3,000 more and hired a trading schooner and its crew to help him salvage the airplanes. Once he got the planes back to the States, Joe had them overhauled. When he offered the planes for sale they were snapped up in two days. Joe's net profit for his hobby work during one vacation was $68,000!

Keep Expanding Your Horizons

Joe J. rested a few weeks after he sold the salvaged planes. What could he do next, he asked himself. Turning back to his air histories, Joe decided to expand his searches to the English Channel countries—Britain, France, Holland, etc. Many times a plane which made an emergency landing would be pushed into a large barn and forgotten. Or a plane which crashed into the sea might be partially revealed at low tide.

With these thoughts in mind, Joe contacted overseas historical groups interested in vintage aircraft. Then, he:

(1) Advertised for people interested in joining him on an expense- and profit-sharing basis

(2) Set up a small company in each country

(3) Outlined his plan of action to each partner

(4) Started a search on land and sea for American, British, German, and Italian aircraft

Joe got his European business started without investing a cent. How? By using the expense money put up by his overseas partners. Of course, Joe has to give his partners a share of the profits. But he doesn't have to make any profit distribution until a profit is earned. However, when you have a profit, you find it much easier to pay out some of it—particularly when you haven't put up a cent to earn yours.

Borrow from Your Partners

Earlier I mentioned a number of advantages of doing business overseas. One big advantage that many beginning wealth builders overlook is the possibility of borrowing money from their overseas contacts.

Many of the thousands of firms listed in *Worldwide Riches Opportunities*, the book described earlier in this chapter, will lend you money once you have a business deal going. Since there are some 2,500 firms listed in the book, you have almost unlimited opportunity to borrow any amount from $100 to $1,000,000, or more.

Joe J. did just this when he discovered several bombers stuck in the sands of the English Channel. With the help of two firms, which lent him $500,000, Joe raised and repaired 24 war planes. His profit on this one deal was more than $200,000. And his partners earned an excellent return on their money too! So don't overlook the big-money opportunities available to you in both the overseas and domestic markets.

Give the Public What It Wants

Every business has a public of some kind. Your public might be just a few companies when you're selling an industrial product. Or you might have millions of customers when you're selling to the general public. Either way, though, your greatest profits occur when you give your public what it wants.

The music recording business is a good example of giving the public what it wants. Here are two examples of what can be done in the field of popular music.

- A housewife invested some $400 in recording her children's singing. This, and her following records, were soon selling several hundred thousand copies. Within a short time after her start in business she was offered $5 million for her company.
- An automobile production line worker borrowed $700 to start a rock recording company. Within ten years his firm was doing $30 million in business.

You can build your business to a healthy, flourishing firm by starting with borrowed money and giving the public what it wants—be your public only a few hundred or many million. Analyze what is wanted by *your* public. Then devise a product or service that serves this want. Using this approach, you can't go wrong if you keep trying.

Build Your Loans to a Great Fortune

You can do it—yes, you can! You can build your loans to a great fortune. Remember:

Borrowing money is not wrong. Millions of businessmen borrow money every year. Why shouldn't you?

The profit potential available to you when using OPM is enormous. When you borrow money you build up greater energy to work to pay it back. This added energy ensures your success.

So start—right now—to build your wealth using OPM. Millions of other people have done it—so can you because you're as capable as any of them. And from one wealth builder to another—*Good Luck!*

HELPFUL MONEY BOOKS

Following are a number of useful books that will help you find sources of business capital, develop business leads, buy a business, etc. If you have the time, I suggest that you study one or more of these books. You will find that your study will pay off in big, rich profits. For, as Aldous Huxley said. "Every man who knows how to read has it in his power to magnify himself, to multiply the ways in which he exists, to make his life full, significant, and interesting."

Business Capital Sources, $15, IWS Inc., P. O. Box 186, Merrick, N. Y. 11566. Hundreds of names and addresses of lenders—banks, finance companies, insurance companies, private firms, etc.—interested in lending up to 100 percent on many business, real-estate, and other projects. Also covers Small Business Administration loans, and going public.

Worldwide Riches Opportunities: 2500 Great Leads for Making Your Fortune in Overseas Trade Without Leaving Home; $25, IWS Inc., P. O. Box 186, Merrick, N. Y. 11566. Lists names and addresses of thousands of firms throughout the world that want to buy hundreds of thousands of different U. S. products. Also listed are hundreds of overseas firms offering saleable imports, and hundreds of overseas firms wanting to be sales representatives (at no charge) for U.S. firms. Many of the firms listed will lend money or extend credit on business deals.

Securities Regulation Guide, $39.50, Prentice-Hall, Inc., Englewood Cliffs, N.J. 07632. Comprehensive guide to operating your company as a corporation. Provides clear-cut, easy-to-understand answers to a variety of questions you might meet when borrowing money, issuing stock, or making a public stock offering.

Acquiring and Merging Businesses, by J. H. Hennessy, Jr., $19.95, Prentice-Hall, Inc., Englewood Cliffs, N.J. 07632. Tells you how to find, screen, and acquire companies using borrowed money, treasury cash, the stock of your own company, etc. Use this guide and you'll learn where to look for acquisition candidates, how to measure the value (to you) of companies, tax advantages and disadvantages of six taxable and four non-taxable acquisition transactions, how to execute the acquisition project, etc.

Long-Term Financing, by John F. Childs, $17.95, Prentice-Hall, Inc., Englewood Cliffs, N.J. 07632. This step-by-step guide to managing your company's finances and setting its profit goals covers many topics, including: capital structure, dividend policy, financing program, types of securities, selling senior securities (i.e., bonds and preferred stock), selling common stock, investor relations, profit goals, cost of capital, and tests of good financial management. This helpful book will enable you to plan your business operations so you earn the profit you seek.

Principles of Business Law—Uniform Commercial Code, $9.95, Prentice-Hall, Inc., Englewood Cliffs, N.J. 07632. Covers more than 2,400 topics in easy-to-understand business language without legal jargon. Summaries of important cases that set judicial precedents are presented. In addition, the book has a 500-term glossary listing terms ranging from *abandonment* to *wills.* This is a book that will help you avoid trouble by telling and showing you what to do *before* you take action.

Direct Costing Techniques for Industry, by Sam M. Woolsey, $17.50, Prentice-Hall, Inc., Englewood Cliffs, N.J. 07632. This book shows you how to use the most modern technique for planning, controlling, and building your business profits. When you use direct costing you develop more dependable data for decision making, set up more effective budgets, use labor and materials more efficiently, maximize your operating profits, and know the exact amount of cash flow each order generates in your business.

How to Build a Second-Income Fortune in Your Spare Time, by Tyler G. Hicks, $6.95, Parker Publishing Co., Inc., West Nyack, N.Y. 10994. Hundreds of useful ideas on starting and getting rich in your own business, using OPM. While you're considering this book, you should also read two others by the same author, each available from this publisher at the same price. These books are: *Smart Money Shortcuts to Becoming Rich,* and *How to Start Your Own Business on a Shoestring and Make Up to $100,000 per Year.*

A Complete Guide to Making a Public Stock Offering, by Elmer L. Winter, $16.00, Prentice-Hall, Inc., Englewood Cliffs, N.J. 07632. This is a step-by-step guide for going public; i.e., selling your firm's stock to the public. Using this guide, you should be able to make your stock offering quickly, efficiently, and economically. This big guide covers both Regulation A and full offerings If you're thinking of selling stock to the public, you should have this book on hand.

Tax Guide for Buying and Selling a Business, $17.75, by Stanley Hagendorf, Prentice-Hall, Inc., Englewood Cliffs, N.J. 07632. Gives over 100 examples of typical buying and selling transactions of sole proprietorships, partnerships, and corporations. Shows you how to avoid hidden tax traps that can lead to excessive or unnecessary taxes. If you're thinking of buying a business, you should have a copy of this book.

Index